Published by Kingston Publishers Limited
7-10 Norman Road
Kingston CSO, Jamaica
First published 1997

ISBN 976-625-108-8

Cover design: Michael Green
Book design: IMAGINE CaD
Preliminary material compiled by Ken Jones
Research: Clyde Hoyte
Editor: Leeta Hearne
Photographs from the collection of Lady Bustamante
Manufactured in the United States of America by Blaze I.P.I.

This book has been sponsored by:
The Bustamante Industrial Trade Union; The Carreras Group; CIBC (Ja.) Limited;
Jamaica Producers Group; The National Commercial Bank (Ja.) Limited;
Dr and Mrs Victor Page; Sandals Resorts;
The Shipping Association of Jamaica.

For those who have shared so much
of my life

Hugh Shearer, Phyllis Salmon, Violet Wattley,
Linette Beckford, Evelyn Sangster-Clarke,
Seragh and Effie Lakasingh

Acknowledgements

A life such as that of Lady Bustamante is, inevitably, one in which many individuals and their families, as well as companies and institutions, have played a significant and historic part.

In seeking to gather support for this publication, Kingston Publishers turned to Mr Eddie Shoucair and Mr Seragh Lakasingh who took up the task positively and cheerfully. Their first response came from Mr Ludlow Stewart of the Shipping Association of Jamaica, an organisation which has had perhaps the longest and most historic association with Lady B. and, for almost all its years, the BITU. Next was the Jamaica Producers, that giant in the banana industry, and, as expected, the Carreras Group, which was one of the first large manufacturing establishments to be officially opened by Sir Alex in 1963. Both gave their full support. The BITU itself, which Lady B. has served so long and faithfully, joined in very willingly.

The CIBC (Ja.) Ltd was equally responsive. Lady B. was the bank's first customer when it opened its doors in Jamaica and she has retained a bank account there ever since.

The SuperClubs Group, owned by John and Aida Issa, together with the Issa Foundation, continued the tradition of close friendship between the Issa family and the Bustamantes and the JLP. John has served the party as a Senator.

The National Commercial Bank (Ja.) Ltd which arose out of the Barclay's Dominion and Overseas Bank of the colonial era also responded. Indeed, Lady B. recalled how much this transition had satisfied the Chief. The Bank finally became the largest in Jamaica, setting the pace for the formation of other Jamaican banks such as the Eagle Commercial Bank and the Workers Bank, both forged out of the savings of the little people who are so dear to Lady B.s heart.

The culminating response from the privately operated companies was that of the Sandals Resorts which under Butch Stewart has grown to reflect the aspirations of a country. He and Lady B. have long had a warm friendly relationship. And, finally in this listing, there were Dr and Mrs Victor Page who can only be called friends indeed: loyal, devoted and true.

We at Kingston Publishers thank you sincerely for all your warm support.

Mike Henry

Contents

1

Not by Sudden Flight

TIME AND TIME AGAIN AS I DRIVE through the gates of Bellencita to go to my office at the Bustamante Industrial Trade Union headquarters in Kingston I think how far the journey has been from Westmoreland to Irish Town. I think of the people who travelled with me on that journey and of the Chief who shaped so much of my life.

I came happily into this world on March 8, 1912, in Parson Reid, a tiny, obscure village in Westmoreland. The place was later renamed Reid's Mountain, but it was just as remote as ever. It lies about a mile up the hill from Ashton where I went to school and church and that is probably why Ashton is generally but mistakenly referred to as my place of birth.

Although I know that Ashton was named after an eminent Moravian missionary, the Reverend Samuel Clayton Ashton, who was as involved in establishing schools as he was with his ministry, up to this day, I have never been able to tell how my little district got its name. I believe that it must have been a mark of respect, for parsons in those days were highly regarded. Parson and Head Teacher were held in awe by everyone in the village. It was they who were asked to speak for the villagers, to represent their needs to the 'higher ups' and to settle domestic disputes or disagreements in business.

The 'higher ups' in those days were not so much those in government as those who owned and operated the large estates around most villages in Jamaica. Our district, Parson Reid, sat in the shadow of such huge cattle properties as Leamington, Findlay's Common and

Woodstock. Two others were Enfield and Kew Park, owned by Theodore Williams and his better known brother, Richard (R.F.) Williams.

I was a welcome baby. My mother, Rebecca Blackwood, felt that she had been blessed with a daughter and she chose the name of Gladys for me. My father, Frank Longbridge, was there too, on a visit from his job as an overseer in St Mary, and I have been told that there was celebration in the district when I was born. Being born out of wedlock was not a major issue in rural Jamaica then. What was seen to be of primary importance was that the children of any union should be given good care and guidance by family and friends.

Everyone in the district called my mother Miss Beck and she was known to be an ambitious young person. I was only three years old when she left the district and the island to look for better opportunities abroad. She left me in the care of my grandparents, God-fearing, hard-working people with a close, loving relationship; sharing good and lean times, praying together and staying together. Grandpa and Grandma were an excellent example for the family and others in the village. He was the sturdy protector and provider; the pillar of strength in the home, proud, reliable and respectable. She looked after our growing-up and taught us Christian principles, commanding us to love one another, to respect our neighbours and to fear God.

Two of my aunts, Amy Blackwood and her sister Rachel, lived with Grandmother Mary Blackwood and they also cared for me. Amy, a sickly person, was soon after invited to live with her sister Margaret in America. Rachel, a hard-working farmer, also did dressmaking for women and children in the district. She had a twin sister, Leah. These were the women who helped to shape my early life and they spared no effort in doing so. Aunt Margaret, who had migrated to the United States some years before, had married a Mr James from Ashton and they had two children who were later sent from America to stay with us.

The male influence in my childhood was Grandpa Blackwood who played an important part in my upbringing. I remember him well

– often decked out in clean, well-ironed garments, with a jaunty felt hat and well-polished high-top boots. His ready smile revealed strong white teeth, kept in good condition by his constant chewing of sugar cane which grew all around. Chewing cane during the day and using chewstick to clean the teeth every morning is a wonderful formula for dental care.

Miss Beck kept in touch with us through regular letters. She was supposed to have gone to America, but she had stopped off in Cuba and never went any further. It was there that she met and married Richard Thompson, who was from Holly Hill in Westmoreland. They had four children while they were living in Cuba. When they returned to Jamaica with their family, I continued to live with my grandparents, aunts and cousins because their home had been mine for so long and I was settled in and comfortable there.

The village of Ashton is not easily found on any map of Jamaica, however enlarged. It is as obscure today as it was when I was a child. Still, those of us who call it home are eternally proud of it. Although we may move and stay away for years, we still recall with fondness the days when we wandered in the bush or played under the spreading trees around the yard. Our family owned about twelve acres with grapefruit, coconuts, coffee, cocoa, pimento, jackfruit and, what I liked best, three varieties of mango – Blackie, Number Eleven and the common 'hairy' mango. We had more than one kind of breadfruit, one called 'Banjam', and of course, there was cane, lots of cane.

For me and my cousins, those were times for play and learning. When we were not jumping, skipping or swinging from the branches of a guava tree, we had chores to perform: planting a garden or reaping corn for the 'dumb things', the fowls that gave us eggs and meat, the cows and the pigs. I had my own cow, named 'Red Gal', and at one time I was interested in a goat, but Grandpa disliked goats because they destroy every plant they find edible. I learnt from then the meaning of the Jamaican saying: 'Don't put you goat mout' on me.'

Like most villagers, we had a horse-drawn mill to extract the cane juice. As children we could only watch this procedure from a distance, because it was against the law for anyone under the age of fifteen to be in the mill-yard during the juicing operation. It would be interesting to know what caused that law to be passed. The juice was made into wet sugar to be used in the home or bought by people who would travel by donkey or mule to sell it at Newmarket or Black River. I became familiar with Newmarket because I had to go there often, riding seven miles on horseback to the Post Office, going through Jack Gate on the border between Westmoreland and St Elizabeth. My errand was to collect letters for family and friends and it was there that I met the first Mrs Cleve Lewis, then the Assistant Post Mistress and the mother of seven children.

It wasn't all outside work and play. We had to learn household skills and we had to study as well – read, write or just sit at the feet of our elders to draw from their experience. That was the ritual regardless of the weather. It may seem boring or oppressive to the child of today. but to us it was a way to open up the hidden wonders of a world which we could only imagine. Better still, it served to keep members of the family together and to increase understanding and goodwill among neighbours and friends.

Looking back over fourscore years and more, I feel that the outstanding thing about my village, and perhaps most other places in Jamaica, was – peace. In school we children read about soldiers and we saw pictures of them with guns and cannons, but these things were nonexistent in our lives. Not one of us had ever seen a gun, not even a soldier's or a policeman's uniform. The nearest police station was away in Bethel Town and there was never a reason to call a constable to deal with anyone in the district. I remember the excitement in Ashton when one young man, Constantine Spence, went off to Kingston and returned, proud and 'boasy' in his police tunic and beating the air with a little cane. Some of the older girls were more than pleased. Others giggled and wondered how he would make out if attacked with a 'cookoo macca stick'. For the record, he did make out well. When he retired he had reached the rank of Superintendent in the Force.

There was no radio in the house at Parson Reid, though I well recall a gramophone which had been brought from America by Amy when she returned with Aunt Margaret's two children. We rarely saw a newspaper and got most of our information about the wider world by word of mouth or from letters sent to us from relatives living elsewhere. In the twenties, we learnt of some of the things happening in Jamaica by 'bush telegraph' and hearsay. Even Kingston seemed far away. In truth, we could better relate to what country people were talking about, like the death of a well-known villager or getting better prices for bananas.

Schooling at Ashton was as effective as home-training in the shaping of our characters. Like so many other village children, I attended school in the Moravian Church which doubled as a school house. Classes held under the strict and watchful eye of Teacher Blake, the principal. By coincidence, when he retired, he was succeeded by another Mr Blake, not at all related to him.

Teachers had as much authority over us as did the closest of relatives or friends. They regarded us as their children, not just their students. They could mete out corporal punishment, which not often happened at my school, but was a general form of discipline in elementary and secondary schools. Unruly children were chastised with the 'wild cane' or a strop. For small offences, such as speaking out of turn, the offender was made to stand for about an hour, face to the wall and with one finger on the lips. Any teacher could deliver the punishment, and children knew that it would be better never to mention the matter when they got home.

Life in the hills was no bed of roses. School was about a mile away from home and I had to walk the distance, come rain or shine. Some fortunate children lived on the main road – a stony, pot-holed pathway cut out for horse and buggy carriages. We had to follow a winding track up and down the hillside where the going and coming were even worse. It was dusty when it was dry and dangerously slippery when wet.

Despite the tiresome journeys, the long days going to and fro, and the nights of indifferent lamplight, I managed to concentrate on class work and homework. I also found time to become a Ranger in the Girl Guide Movement which was headed by Miss Findlay, the local property owner's daughter.

I even became quite an accomplished player of the organ. It was the head teacher's daughter, Irene, who taught me the rudiments of music. She did so well that in a short time I was playing at Sunday School and at Church services in the absence of the organist, who was sister to Constantine Spence. I must have been about eleven years old at the time and I can well remember Irene Blake saying to me, "Gladys, I have never had a student who took in music as fast as you did. Keep up the good work, my child. You have a far way to go."

I don't know how far my teacher expected me to go, but where organ music is concerned I didn't go much further than the Church or my own living room. But I have always played and my home has never been without an instrument to satisfy my love for music.

Although my young life was full of so much activity, I never neglected my formal education. It was my priority. There were none of the wonderful opportunities provided for children nowadays. Nor were there any of the magnetic temptations and distractions which students today must resist in order to learn anything of real value. So I studied hard, spurred on by the knowledge that there was no other way to success in life or to reach such ambitious heights of employment as teaching or nursing. I pored over the books, I asked questions and applied myself diligently to all my subjects.

Everybody knew how seriously I took the memory gem from the poet Longfellow that was drilled into our ears at school:

The heights by great men reached and kept
Were not attained by sudden flight,
But they, while their companions slept,
Were toiling upward in the night.

Many a night and many a day that gem kept going round in my

head. I felt as though I was being shaped for a life of usefulness to others as well as myself. I realised, too, that the preparation for such a role would not be easy. The result would come by studious and diligent application, not by sudden flight.

There were many other memory gems that we had to learn by heart. Another favourite of mine was:

Do all the good you can,
In all the ways you can,
To all the people you can,
Just as long as you can.
Love the old if you are young,
Help the weak if you are strong;
Keep a guard upon your tongue,
Own a fault if you are wrong.

I often quoted those verses, and I tried to live by them, so nobody in the village was surprised when I finished the course and passed the Second Jamaica Local Examination. This achievement motivated me to reach for even better things. It also qualified me to work as a pupil teacher in the school and I proudly accepted that post at the princely salary of sixteen shillings a month.

At face value, my 1928 pay was equal to less than two dollars a month today. However, it was good money at that time. I could buy a nice pair of shoes for nine shillings and sixpence, stockings, a dress and a hat, and still have money to spare. Today you can't buy half a loaf of bread with the amount of cash that kept me happy for a month. As a matter of fact, the last time I checked, one single slice of hard-dough bread was costing just about two dollars.

The role of pupil teacher gave me some new insights to the ways of school children. It made me very interested in youth training and since then I have had a deep love for young people. I never had any children of my own, but I have raised many over the years and I have been godmother to more I also discovered that the love of imparting knowledge to children was one thing but another was the stern supervision which I received as a trainee teacher. That taught me a lot that I was to use in the future.

Memories of Ashton and Parson Reid seem so simple now. Yet I can see how some of these ordinary experiences prepared me for a course in life which I could not even imagine at that time. I cannot tell precisely at what age I was, but I do know that early in my life I had this feeling that I wanted to be somebody who would benefit people – people like those among whom I grew up. Some of them looked for a better life in towns nearby or as far away as Kingston. Others stayed and tried their hand at whatever limited opportunities the countryside had to offer. Men could only look forward to working on the estates, chopping cane or rising to the grade of foreman; carrying bananas or hoping to be a tallyman at the banana ports. Women aspired to teaching, nursing or keeping house for others; and some had nothing to do. There were walls on many sides, but it is important to remember that although one cannot always climb over obstacles one can always patiently walk around them.

Early in 1930 I reached the first major crossroads in my life. I had to choose between my beloved Ashton and the strange city of Kingston. Ever since I had passed my exams, I had been pressured by my elders and my friends to seek out more learning and also employment, which could only be found in Kingston. I resisted the advice for a while, but the gentle persuasion continued. They wanted me to know that going to Kingston was, if nothing else, a sign of one's ambition and self-confidence. But the thought of leaving the comfort and security of familiar surroundings for the challenges of the city was not appealing.

Then Aunt Amy returned from the United States, bringing with her Aunt Margaret's two daughters, Doris and Phyllis, to be looked after by Aunt Rachel, who had her own daughter, also named Phyllis. Aunt Amy wanted me to further my studies by attending a high school and so she tried her best to arouse my interest in more education. She often told me about the exciting places in America – the bright lights of New York City, the tall buildings, the factories and the well-paying jobs, the big schools and the great colleges. It seemed that all these were for the taking and that high school and Kingston were stepping stones to that land of opportunity.

Finally, I gave in. One nice warm day, I packed my grip, bade my friends and most of my relatives good-bye and set off on the journey to Kingston where I would be boarding with a Mrs Margaret Gooden in Jones Town. But I was not travelling alone. Aunt Amy's hope for me was about to be realised and she was happy to travel with me and see me settled in. My Aunt Rachel and Uncle Jim, who was the only boy out of sixteen children in his family, came along as well for the trip.

Getting from the village of Parson Reid to the city of Kingston was no pleasure trip. There was no bus, taxi, buggy or motor car. Nobody in the district owned a bicycle to give anyone a 'tow'. Even if there had been a bike, the tracks were too rough for travelling in such luxury. The train for Kingston ran from Catadupa in St James, but to get to that railway station we had to choose between walking the whole six miles, going by horseback or riding a donkey with hampers on either side. My dignified aunt decided that riding a horse was best. Never mind the suitcase which had to be carried not so much by hand as by head. There were always villagers ready and willing to walk with us and to share the load, and this important trip was no exception.

It took about four hours to get to Catadupa and what a relief it was to buy my ticket and board that train for the long haul. I was very tired by the time I sat down on the wooden seat. That and the acrid smoke that belched from the engine made it difficult to relax and what made me even more restless were the questions that kept rising in my mind. How would I like Kingston? What would school be like? Would I find a job and settle down or would I hurry back to the comfort of my old home? As I pondered, I kept remembering the touching folk song about Eva.

In those days one popular way of travelling from the country to Kingston was to follow the train line on foot. Eva, so the story goes, had become tired of living in the remote hills and decided to escape by following the train line the long walk to Kingston. But she soon became tired of city life and hurried back home to get a teasing from her friends and the nickname 'Follow line gal'. If you have ever heard that song performed by my friend Olive Lewin and her colleagues in the Jamaican Folk Singers, you will get a good idea of how I felt at sixteen, leaving home for the first time, going to Kingston and thinking about how:

Eva falla line gone; Eva run come back; Eva!
Eva falla line gone; Eva run come back; Eva!
Eva falla line gone; Eva run come back;
What a gwine to do with that 'falla line gal', Eva!

Eva walk go a Kingston; Eva run come back; Eva!
Eva walk go a Kingston; Eva run come back; Eva!
Eva walk go a Kingston; Eva run come back;
What a gwine to do with that 'falla line gal', Eva!

Dem put Eva in a bed; Eva could not sleep; Eva!
Dem put Eva in a bed; Eva could not sleep; Eva!
Dem put Eva in a bed; Eva could not sleep;
Put her on the floor, Eva sleep like engine, Eva!

As Eva's song kept running through my head, the train sped along through the countryside, stopping at every station. Finally, we reached the plains of Kingston. As I walked out of the station it struck me that I had never seen so much open space with so few trees, so many houses in one place and so many people out in public. Kingston was fascinating. Around me were the busy streets and lanes, and out in the distance the hills of St Andrew. Then southward was the Caribbean Sea of which I had read and heard but had never seen.

Miss G. in her early Kingston days

2

Toiling Upward

WHAT A DIFFERENCE THERE WAS BETWEEN MY VILLAGE and the big city of Kingston. And not just the look of the city: the people seemed different too – the way they dressed, the way they walked and the way they spoke made me feel that country people and city people were often distances apart not only in miles but in their ways as well. Yet it didn't take me long to notice that there were certain similarities since many 'Kingstonians' had really come from the country parishes and had kept in close contact with the families they had left behind.

In those days, people in the 'country parts' used to send baskets, bags or boxes of foodstuff to their relatives in the city. That was the traditional generosity of rural folk, and no self-respecting country man or woman would think of arriving in the city with just their 'two long hands'. They had to come bearing gifts, whether in a crocus bag slung over the shoulder or a carton balanced atop the head.

Trucks came in weekly all the way from the rural parishes, even from as far as Westmoreland, carrying higglers and their goods to the markets in the western part of Kingston. And it was there that many city dwellers would 'meet' the driver or sideman to collect supplies sent by their country relatives to Solas Market at the corner of Orange and West Queen Streets and Chigger Foot Market at the corner of Princess and Heywood Streets. Then there was Coronation Market, at Darling Street and Spanish Town Road. Named in commemoration of the crowning of King George the VI of England, it was popularly known as Duppy Market because it had been established on the site of an old cemetery. Redemption Ground, at the corner of Princess and West

Queen Streets, was open on Saturday mornings for the display and sale of goods seized by bailiffs. People went there to redeem their goods; and so the place got its name. Nearby there were the 'grass-yards', where no grass grew. The drays and donkey carts would be taken there together with the grass brought to feed the animals resting for the return journey. Coal, really charcoal, was sold in the grass yards, which might sound strange, but since most of the coal used in Kingston came from the country in these drays, the yards were the most convenient places to make the sales.

Week by week, the trucks, and later 'country buses' helped to increase the population of Kingston. Large numbers of the younger people travelled to the city in search of work and opportunities for better living. Many who had no relatives to accommodate them, lodged near the market while they searched for 'live-in' employment. Inevitably, population density increased in the area stretching westward from Princess Street.

Workers from the country were generally regarded as being more reliable, hard-working and docile than Kingstonians. Because of this, employers from the suburbs of Kingston were always on the look-out for 'domestic servants late from the country'. On the other hand, clerical, commercial or professional types were not expected to be found coming from the rural areas. In fact, those job opportunities were limited in Kingston, even for men; and so most young women, especially black young women, had to set their sights on the already open gates leading to the traditional occupations for women such as sewing, teaching and nursing. Those who wanted to break out of these confines, had to study twice as hard and run twice as fast as the ones with more modest ambitions.

Because I had enjoyed teaching so much, I had visions of going to a teachers' college, graduating and helping to shape the lives of the young, preparing them for the challenges of the future. However, this was not a practical possibility and so I chose instead to train in commercial subjects. It was clear to me that education could make a profound difference to my life, and I decided to pursue it with dedication and determination.

Tutorial Secondary and Commercial College on Duke Street was a leading school among those offering commercial subjects. I heard that it had a good reputation for producing well-educated youngsters and time has told the story of many who left an indelible mark on the Jamaican scene. One outstanding example is Wesley Powell who, as a young man, started his own small school which gradually grew into the impressive complex now known as Excelsior Education Centre. When I was entering Tutorial, Wesley was in his final year.

While I was at Tutorial College, many other strong and lasting friendships were formed which were to help me in future years. Apart from Wesley Powell, there were Alvin Henry, founder of Durham College of Commerce, Roy McNeil, who would become a Minister of Health after Independence, and Ivy Bailey. Other friends included Glen Owen who would later be a long-serving Principal of Mico Training College, Edith Nelson and Marion Bravo who, like myself, would work in the trade union movement. Edith retired from the BITU after many long years and Marion, though past the age of seventy, is still there looking after the accounts. Another long-lasting friend was James Rose Lloyd who joined the Civil Service and had a notable career. After he retired from the post of Administrator of Grenada, he became Assistant Secretary in the Prime Minister's Office, while Bustamante was in office. He often accompanied us on official visits overseas.

I have mentioned the coincidence of my two head teachers at Ashton being named Blake. Oddly enough, at Tutorial the Principal was another Mr Blake – Roderick Jardine Blake. He and his first wife, Doris May, operated the school. He was born in St Elizabeth and, like his father, he was a graduate of Mico Training College. Before becoming a co-founder and principal of Tutorial, he had taught at Darliston in my native Westmoreland and had reached the rank of Elementary Schoolmaster at the age of twenty-one. He was my inspiration.

What would later prove to be another coincidence was my choice of a school on Duke Street, a road that was to play an important role in my life in Kingston. My school was at 121½ Duke Street and my place of worship was the Moravian Church of the Redeemer, at the corner of Duke and North Streets. My pastor was the Right Reverend John Kneale who, in 1942, became Bishop of the Moravian Church in Jamaica. At that time, the head churches of the Christian denominations were located in Kingston except for the Anglican Cathedral which was and still is in Spanish Town.

Also in those times, and for many years afterwards, all the traditional church leaders in Jamaica were men from overseas. The head Anglican bishop was Australian-born, the Moderator of the Presbyterian Kirk was Scottish, the Roman Catholic Bishop was American, the Commander of the Salvation Army was English and the head of the Methodists was Welsh. In addition, the Secretary of the YMCA was English and the Secretary of the YWCA was Scottish. There was no significant change until 1947 when the Reverend Percival Gibson, Headmaster of Kingston College, was appointed the Anglican Suffragan Bishop of Kingston. Later he was appointed the first Jamaican Lord Bishop of Jamaica.

Even then I had an interest in church work and I noticed that the City Mission, founded in Kingston, was growing and reaching out to other parishes from its headquarters at Blount Street in western Kingston. This religious organisation broke early from tradition by having a woman, the Reverend Mary Louise Coore, as its Bishop. She was a co-founder of the movement in 1929 and, as a respected leader, was a fine role model for young black women. The fact that she celebrated her birthday on March 9, a day after mine, gave me a little extra pride and a further incentive to do well at school.

I had come to Kingston with a good grounding in the subjects taught in Elementary School, so I was able to concentrate on acquiring the skills of accounting, shorthand and typewriting. I also studied Spanish and continued with music; and I was well rewarded for my scholastic endeavours. My main instructor was Mr Alvin Henry, who later founded Durham College of Commerce as well as a thriving furniture manufacturing business. He was a good teacher and before long

I was able to write at speeds of 120 to 150 words a minute in shorthand and quite fast on the old Remington typewriter on which we practiced. When time for the examinations came, Mr Henry suggested that, in spite of my known speed, I should take the test for 120 words per minute and combine it with typewriting. They called that combination 'Amanuensis'. The dictionary described it as 'a slave with secretarial duties'. I called it 'easy', took the exam and passed comfortably. That certificate is, to this day, one of my prized possessions.

Armed with a strong basic education, musical talent, my new skills and fresh ideas, I felt that I was ready for a triumphant return to Ashton. But before doing so, I decided to stay for a while to find out more about Kingston and its opportunities. Besides, I wanted to be able to tell friends and family as much as I could about the big city – a seemingly exciting place to them!

Something I had already discovered that surprised me was that although for most of Kingston, just as in the country, Saturday was the busiest day of the week, the main city streets were almost deserted. The reason was that whole blocks of businesses and stores on these streets were owned by Jewish families who observed Saturday as their Sabbath. That was their quiet time. For others, Sunday was the day of worship and the time for rest and recreation. Young and old would take the tramcars or walk to Hope Gardens or Rockfort Gardens. Many families made it a habit to take a Sunday evening stroll together.

Thinking about those peaceful days, I sometimes marvel at how much Kingston has changed. The beautiful Hope River has been transformed into something like a rock garden. Once it had such a good flow of water that hundreds of people would go to bathe by its banks at Papine. Its cool, clear water ran from the hills near Newcastle, traversing the gorge behind the Wareika to reach the sea at a point on the road to St Thomas. In the years since I first knew it, the water has steadily decreased to the point where the lower reaches came to be known as the Dry River.

Another Sunday occupation was reading the *Daily Gleaner* although it was not published on that day. I learnt that this was because the publication was also owned by Jewish families, mainly the DeCordovas and the Ashenheims. Since they were observing the Sabbath from Friday evening to Saturday evening, there was no *Gleaner* on Sundays. Readers would buy the Saturday newspaper and set it aside for leisurely Sunday reading. Incidentally, the *Gleaner* had a weekend magazine section even way back then. There being no colour photos or colour printing in newspapers in those days, the magazine section was printed on pink newsprint and was often referred to as the pink pages.

I cannot recall any serious or sustained newspaper writing that would have drawn attention to the plight of the poor. Still, there were stirrings in the air by the time the thirties were half-way through and gradually things began to happen as more and more people were giving expression to their feelings. The principal voice on behalf of the masses in the early thirties was, of course, Marcus Garvey. However, when he wrote about the problems in Jamaica, the Colonial Office in London would be officially informed that the scene was not as bad as the pictures he tended to paint. Time would prove that he was right.

A major form of entertainment was music. At that time, people made their own music. There was no local radio station and few homes had a gramophone but there were many singers and musicians in Kingston. I heard more of those performing in the churches rather than in the concert hall. A great Jamaican tenor was Granville Campbell who not only sang beautifully but also wrote songs, played the piano and composed the Festival Mass to celebrate the Golden Jubilee of the Roman Catholic Bishop, Thomas Emmet. For obvious reasons, it was the organists that held my attention. There were such outstanding performers as Edgerton Andrews at the Kingston Parish Church, George Goode, conductor, organist and choirmaster at St Michael's Anglican Church at Victoria Avenue and Lindsay Bruce, organist and choirmaster, who drew big crowds to his cantatas at

Scot's Kirk on Duke Street. Among other virtuosos on the organ were Arthur Chevolleau at Holy Trinity Cathedral, William Aldred at the Anglican Cathedral in Spanish Town and Herbert East Dodd who played the organ at St George's Anglican Church on East Street for over sixty years.

I particularly remember one singer who had an exceptionally powerful soprano voice. I heard it first one Sunday morning while I was walking past Kingston Parish Church. So impressive was the singing that people were going into the churchyard to get a glimpse of the artiste who was taking those high notes with unusual clarity and power. I joined the curious onlookers, peeped in at the door and, lo and behold, the soprano was a grown man. It was Mr John Lyons, a noted singer from his childhood. At puberty his voice did not change and at forty he was still singing soprano, and with more power than any female voice. He migrated to England around the late 1940s and it is said that on one occasion the British Broadcasting Corporation had scheduled a programme of classical music in which the famous Australian soprano, Joan Sutherland, was to take part. At the last moment, the great lady was unable to fulfil the engagement and Johnny Lyons, then in London, was hurriedly summoned as a substitute. To the astonishment of everyone, he competently filled the gap, without much rehearsal, performing some difficult high-pitched arias with the greatest of ease.

Kingston was an exciting place in those quiet days, especially for a country girl like me, but finally it was time to go home. I was anxious to put my experiences to work, to make a meaningful contribution to my own community and also to improve my own development. And I missed the familiar faces at home. Underlying all this was my longing for the people and the places where I had spent my happy childhood. Family and friends welcomed me warmly on my return and I was treated in much the same way as the prodigal child of the New Testament. I revelled in the extra attention and I was thrilled that my neighbours seemed satisfied with what they saw as my great success.

But I soon began to feel bored and dissatisfied with the empty daylight hours, the dark nights and the seeming hopelessness of country life.

I was ready to work, but at Parson Reid and nearby Ashton there was very little to which I could put my hand and my brain. I had to look outside the district to where the opportunities lay, and I looked towards Montego Bay. I went to visit my friends, Willie and Esther Anglin, who invited me to stay with them at their home at Orange District, near Sign. I have always been grateful for their generosity which made it possible for me to meet a lot of new people and to discover a new town.

Memories of my stay in Montego Bay during the early 1930s, come back to me vividly. Armed with my shorthand and typewriting skills, I made the rounds of lawyers' offices, the United Fruit Company, the Telephone Company, retail stores, shops and restaurants. These places formed the core of the main business district running parallel to the coast on land rising almost abruptly into the hills forming the eastern boundary of the town. My search for gainful occupation ended when I found employment at a relatively small business place operated by Mr Saleem Simmons in Market Street.

Mr Simmons ran a store named Havana Sports and he employed me to work on Saturdays. This allowed me time to move about Montego Bay and to develop a vision of the change I longed to see in my own circumstances and also in the everyday lives of many others who situation seemed to cry out for something better. I am sure that what I witnessed of the conditions of work on the wharves in Montego Bay aroused my interest in port workers and, eventually, in all categories of workers, for the rest of my life.

Montego Bay was a banana port in those days and shipments took place every week. When the banana boats could not dock alongside the wharves, they remained in the middle of the harbour.

Large lighters, with oars handled by strong men, took the fruit from wharf-side to the ships. All day the trucks would come in from large and small farms in the western parts of the island; and when the truck side-men had unloaded the bananas near the street entrance to the wharf, most of the work of loading the lighters was done by women.

Those women seemed to be as strong as any man. Their working clothes were old and covered with the stains from the bananas they carried. Large pockets sewn onto the front of their skirts held the tickets they received for each bunch they bore upon their heads. With each delivery they would shout to the 'tallyman' so that he could check the quantities received from the different farms.

Work on the wharves went on day and night when the ships were in and I heard the workers sing the 'Tallyman' folk song with its chorus of 'Day deh light an' me waan go home' long before it became a lasting commercial success. And it is one that has perpetuated a lasting misunderstanding as a result of 'Six-han', seven-han', eight-han', bunch!' being changed to 'Six-foot, seven-foot, eight-foot, bunch. . . ' We have even had many Jamaican singers slavishly repeating the error.

As most Jamaicans well know, bananas grow on long stems in what we call 'hands'. (To make things more complicated, these are what are called bunches in other countries) On each 'hand' the separate bananas are described as 'fingers'. The whole growth is known as a 'bunch' or 'stem', which can have any number of 'hands'. An interesting example of worker exploitation can be seen in the old practice of the big banana-shipping companies that bought bananas by the stem from small farmers. According to their system, a stem did not qualify as a bunch unless it had a minimum of nine hand; so when an eight-hand stem was delivered, the farmer had to supply a second stem to make up a 'count bunch'. However, if the farmer supplied a thirteen-hand stem it would still be regarded as one 'count bunch'.

Week after week this system grieved our farmers and over and over again this exploitation would be hotly debated by the Jamaica Agricultural Society. But it remained unchanged until many years later when the buying system was changed to boxing and purchase by weight.

While I was in Montego Bay I became conscious of the divided social structure there. It did exist in Kingston too but not so blatantly. At that time, you could not spend two days in Montego Bay without noticing that prejudice was dominant amongst the population. Apart from colour prejudice, which even affected persons of similar shades of complexion, there were divisions based on all sorts of strange ideas. Although the town was quite small, there were two Anglican churches about three minutes' walk from each other. The Parish Church of St James was located on large grounds in Church Street and Trinity Anglican Church was then at the busy bustling corner of Barnett Street and St James Street. St James was High Church, with services closely resembling the Roman Catholic Mass, while Trinity was Low Church and held very plain and simple services.

There was hardly a dark face to be seen amongst the workers in the stores or offices in the centre of the town. Certainly, there was none in either of the two banks – Barclays and Nova Scotia. Black business people were few and far between. They were druggists who ran their own establishments, tailors, shoe-makers, fishermen and small shopkeepers. I remember two black photographers in the town and, as there were few laundries, women took in washing as a good way of earning a livelihood. Black people were mostly in business in the two markets. One was on Market Street, just behind the Court House, and the other was the meat and fish market at the corner of Creek Street and St James Street.

The dry goods stores were owned by Lebanese and Syrians, mainly of the large Marzouca family. Chinese business people concentrated on grocery shops, and East Indians, such as the Dadlanis, had one or two dry goods stores. Walter Fletcher, an Englishman, who had been in Montego Bay since 1917, operated the largest insurance agency in those parts and he also owned a wharf attached to his premises on Harbour Street, from which bananas were exported weekly. On St James Street, the Jewish family headed by Samuel Hart operated one of the larger hardware stores as well as the Ethelhart Hotel, the most prominent building in the town, sitting on the first hill rising from close to the sea at the northern end of St James Street. Another hardware store was run by the DeLissers who made the larger part of their income by operating several farm properties in St James and adjoining parishes.

Those DeLisser enterprises were run by the brothers Clifford and Oscar, but it was Clifford who was the most dynamic. It was said that he rose at 3 a.m. daily to 'think quietly'. A story was told about how he did not like to see a piece of idle land on any of his properties. One day while he was inspecting one of their properties, he spotted a piece with nothing but bush on it. He demanded of his overseer, "What is that place doing without a crop growing on it?" The overseer replied,"But Mass Clifford, that piece is not part of our land." And Clifford promptly responded,"Well, buy it and put it to work."

Then there was also the Barnett Sugar Estate and its factory, owned by the very well-known Kerr-Jarrett family. The estate provided much employment for all categories of workers.

Most of the lawyers and other professionals practising in Montego Bay were either white or of very light complexion. However, there were two black doctors who were very highly regarded and quite prosperous. One of them, Dr Alexander Apfel Vernon, acquired a large property called John's Hall, east of Barnett Estate on the road to Maroon Town. He also had an imposing residence on Union Street.

Dr Vernon had been one of a small group of doctors who were in the habit of going to the beach in the early mornings to bathe where a mineral spring emptied into the sea through a rocky cave some distance north of the town centre. This practice had led to the place becoming known as Doctors' Cave. In time, the Doctors' Cave Club developed a fine reputation as a bathing resort, but in the mid-1930s if you asked the people who ran the Club to name the doctors who gave the place its name, you would hear of Dr Culver and Dr Alexander McCatty, but hardly ever the name of Dr Vernon, because he was black. Such was the prejudice that if a black person swam down the adjoining Cornwall Beach and happened to put foot on the sands of Doctors' Cave, some of the white swimmers would come out of the water and quickly depart.

Not only blacks but also, strangely enough, the Chinese were denied membership at the exclusive Doctors' Cave. In fact, in its early days, women were not welcome within its precincts as it was considered to be a men's club. After a while, however, women were allowed to use the facilities between the hours of 1.30 and 3.30 in the afternoon, at which times men were required to absent themselves.

At the western fringe of Barnett Estate, at the southern end of the town, was a black-sand beach called River Bay. That was where Montego Bay's black residents could freely swim. There was also Cornwall Beach, owned by a group of black Montegonians who, at one point, came to the conclusion that the fence separating their beach from Doctors' Cave was in the wrong position, giving Doctors' Cave more than its rightful share of waterfront. Their appeals to the Doctors' Cave management went unheeded, so one night they simply moved the fence themselves. This night-time escapade had been well-organised by the Hon. Philip Lightbody, the Member of the Legislative Council for St James, who got together some young men from the poorer section of town for his daring purpose. The next night the Doctors' Cave people returned the fence to its former position; and this shifting back and forth went on for some time until a search of the records of the Parochial Board produced a document which seemed to settle the dispute by showing that the disputed territory should be divided in half.

The other black doctor in Montego Bay, Herbert L. Morrison, enjoyed a large practice and also owned a substantial dwelling on Market Street. People who knew these two black doctors well, were never tired of praising their skill. They were of different generations but their reputations were equally high. Dr Vernon was the older man and his children, like himself, served Jamaica very well. One son, Willie Vernon, became chairman of the Parochial Board of St James and later was the first Mayor of Montego Bay. A daughter of his became the wife of the noted Anglican

Lady B.'s mother, Rebecca Thompson

Gladys Longbridge's Christmas Greetings card in 1934

Two little girls and life-long friends of Lady B., Edith Nelson (l.) and Marion Bravo. They joined Miss G. at the BITU soon after it was formed and served it for many years.

Miss G. and her bicycle in 1946

Miss G. in her early Kingston days

Miss G. at the typewriter at the Richmond Hill Inn in Montego Bay in 1947, typing up the Chief's notes for the Montego Bay Conference on the proposed Federation of the West Indies.

Mr Cyril Mallett, a loyal and devoted officer of the BITU in the early days.

Sir Alexander and Miss G. disembarking from their ship in Kingston after attending the Coronation of Queen Elizabeth II in 1953

In London (on a windy day) with the Chief on their 1951 visit

Tucker Avenue. Surprise birthday party for Sir Eric, Chief Minister of Grenada.
Second from the left, Roy McNeil; 2 and 3, Dr and Mrs Lloyd;
8, The Chief; seated at the table, Eric Gairy; 11, Mrs Ronald Irvine;
12, Madame Rose Leon; 14, Mr Leon; 16. Miss G.

Miss G. in 1952

The Chief in a relaxed moment on board ship

On board the Queen Mary sailing from London to New York

Sir Alex and Miss G. being greeted by the Governor of New York after visiting Jamaican farm workers in Connecticut. At left,. Mr (later Sir) Herbert MacDonald and Minister of Agriculture, Isaac Barrant. 1954.

With Lady Morley, wife of the first British High Commissioner to Jamaica, on the occasion of the opening of the Carreras Tobacco Factory at Twickenham Park, Spanish Town. This was the first major industrial enterprise established in Jamaica after Independence.

Lady B. with film star Ginger Rogers who visited Jamaice in 1962

Sir Alex and Lady B. about to board the flight to London to attend the 1962 Commonwealth Prime Ministers Conference

Sir Alexander and Lady B. on their way to attend a dinner party at Buckingham Palace, London 1962

Returning from John F.Kennedy's funeral in Washington in 1963. From the left: Noel Crosswell, Commissioner of Police; Clement Tavares; Hugh Shearer; Wilton Hill; Chief of Staff, JDF, David Smith; and Edward Seaga.

Viewing the body of the late Ken Jones, Minister of Communications and Works, at the Friends Church in Hector's River, Portland, 1964.

Miss Edith Nelson speaking at a dinner in honour of Sir Alex.

1963 Youth Rally at the National Stadium. From the left: Ranny Williams; Abe Issa; Minister Edward Seaga; Lady B.; Mrs Aaron Matalon.

Lady B. addressing a JLP Conference at the National Arena

Lady B. escorts Her Majesty Queen Elizabeth II up the steps into Jamaica House, 1966

Queen Elizabeth II and Prince Philip enjoying a conversation with Sir Alex

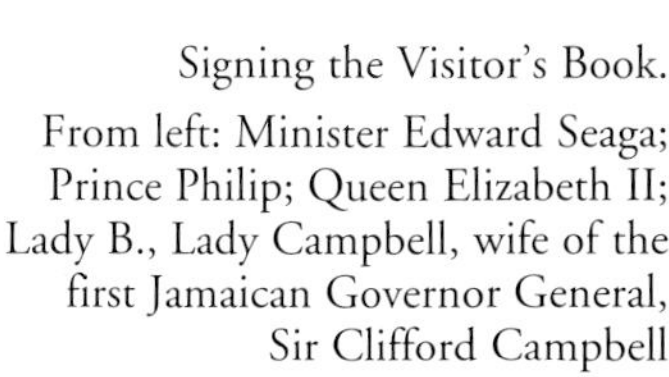

Signing the Visitor's Book.

From left: Minister Edward Seaga; Prince Philip; Queen Elizabeth II; Lady B., Lady Campbell, wife of the first Jamaican Governor General, Sir Clifford Campbell

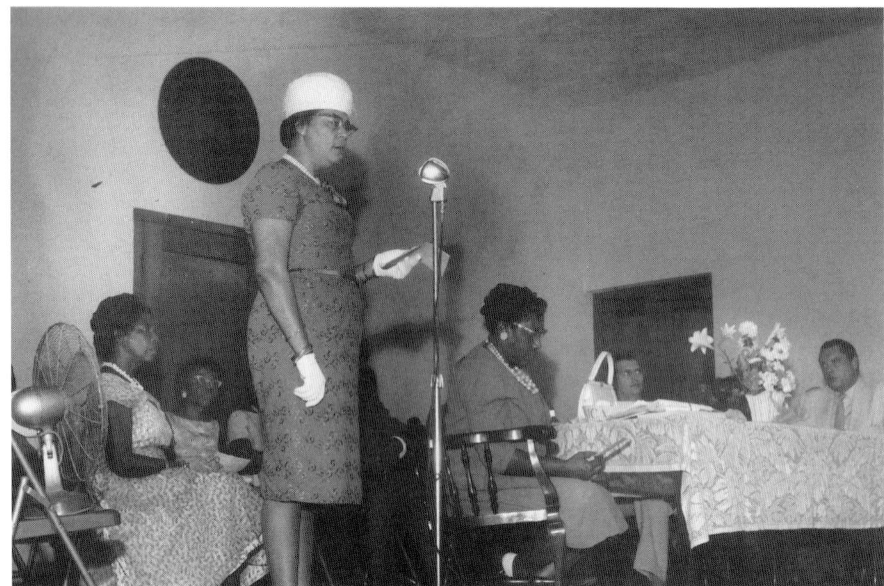

Addressing 240 Trippers, members of the Moravian Church, leaving on an educational tour of North America, 1964.

Meeting schoolgirls

priest, Canon R.O.C. King whose son is Ambassador Peter King. Their daughter, Angela, has had an outstanding career in the United Nations Organisation and is now a UN Assistant Secretary General

Today Montego Bay is described as Jamaica's tourist capital. But in the early 1930s this designation was only slowly 'coming to come'. I understand that it was the beautiful sunsets seen from the waterfront that contributed to the early vision of the place as a tourist resort. A well-known English chiropractor, Sir Herbert Barker, became impressed with the scene and began to spread the word in Britain that Montego Bay was a place where one's energies could be restored during the winter months.

Then someone else came and sat at the same spot from which Sir Herbert had gazed. This time it was a Jamaican woman, Mrs May Belle Ewen, daughter of a Custos of Westmoreland and wife of another Custos. She saw not only the beauty of the view but also a vision of what could be done with that rocky ledge next to Doctors' Cave. She bought the piece of land, gave up the Staffordshire Hotel in Union Street and on her newly-purchased bit of rockstone, built the Casa Blanca Hotel which quickly became known in many countries and set the stage for the development of the winter resort we now know.

Such was the Montego Bay in which I found myself early in 1934. Living there was like a whole new education for me. It was completely unlike the country life of Ashton and Parson Reid and although it was a town it was different from Kingston. I did not like some aspects of its way of life. Sometimes I thought of my precious Amanuensis. What was I doing with it? And often, too, I kept thinking of the workers on the wharves who seemed to have no further to go in life. Could I ever do anything to bring about a change for myself and for those who toiled so hard for so little? At that point at which I realised that a mere cry of despair is not really prayer. I knew then that one had to pray, believing.

I prayed, believing. And the answer came. My Aunt Margaret arrived without warning in Montego Bay and announced that she had come to take me to Kingston. Her husband had died so she had returned from America with her third child. She decided to set up a home at Waltham Park Road in Kingston and had gone to Parson Reid to collect her two older daughters as well as Aunt Rachel and her daughter Phyllis. Hearing that I was in Montego Bay, she had come right over and, after a few preliminary words, said to me, "My girl, I've got to take you out of this bush. You are coming back with me to Kingston."

That was just what I wanted to hear. I jumped at the invitation for I knew that there was a better way and that I had a dream to 'toil upward' and to reach for. So, without returning to Parson Reid, I was off again to the big city in search of my dream. That was on the 10th of March, 1934.

As the train rolled along toward Kingston, I was thankful that my prayer had been answered so unexpectedly. At the same time, I could not help feeling concerned about the uncertainties ahead. Concerned, but not afraid because I was braced by the power of the religious faith that had always given me courage and confidence in whatever I set out to do. So I meditated, asked for divine guidance and rested my faith in God.

It is to my religious upbringing that I owe that faith in God. It has been the shield and armour that have given me courage in the face of every challenge, whether in public or private circumstances. Throughout the years, whenever I have been worried or apprehensive, I have found it useful and rewarding to turn to prayer and my belief in God. I am ever mindful of the wisdom of my guardians who led me to the church. And I feel myself fortunate that the Moravians were so active and influential in my neighbourhood when I was a child. I was baptised by the Reverend J.T. Carnegie, M.M.

The Moravians have a long history in Jamaica. Almost two hundred and fifty years ago, they were the first missionaries to come to Jamaica to work among and teach the slaves. They suffered persecution themselves but persisted in their efforts to establish churches and schools for slaves and, after Emancipation, even communities for ex-slaves.

I grew up reading and listening to stories about these men and women who had braved the demands and dangers of their day. I believed that I was being shaped for a similar life of social service, even involving personal sacrifice. I admired the efforts of such men as Jacob Zorn, whose name is attached to the church at Christiana and Heinrich Gottlieb Pfeiffer who was made to suffer as a result of the Sam Sharpe Rebellion. He was arrested, subjected to severe mental and physical abuse and tried for his life. Fortunately, a large number of witnesses testified on his behalf and he was spared to carry on his noble work for many more years. My Grandpa had a book in which in which Heinrich Pfeiffer and Jacob Zorn were mentioned.

Wherever there was a Moravian congregation there would be a school. One of the first places where this dual operation took place was the district of Lititz in St. Elizabeth which, I believe, got its name from one of the German towns where the church had its beginnings. Lititz School which began in 1823 at Rowe's Corner, on the road to Alligator Pond, is considered to be the oldest primary school in Jamaica. The first public water supply in Jamaica was also established at Lititz where a large public tank was built by a Moravian brother, William A. Prince.

Moravian mission stations spread through western and central Jamaica. Long before I was born, the Beaufort Church reached out to start the church-and-school at Ashton where I got my early schooling, as well as my first lessons in music and sewing. It was not a coincidence when I was thinking of a career as a teacher that I hoped to go to Bethlehem Training College, founded by the Moravians in 1888 to train women teachers. Samuel Ashton, after whom my first school was named, was also Principal of Bethlehem College between 1889 and 1929. They called him Daddy Ashton and later Grandpa. One of his students, Alice Jolly, later married a Westmoreland schoolmaster named Clifford Campbell. We all know them best as Sir Clifford and Lady Campbell, the first Jamaicans to become residents of Kings House.

My gratitude to the Moravians is not confined to the early education which I received at Ashton Church and School. Like so many others from my home district, I owe thanks to the land settlement programme which was introduced by the religious bodies following Emancipation. Many of the former slaves were driven from whatever holdings they might have occupied, or charged impossible rents. The problem was to find lands on which they could become self-sufficient.

It was the religious groups, particularly the Moravians, the Quakers, and the Baptists, which came to the rescue, buying lands from the planters and establishing what came to be known as Free Villages. The Moravians bought a property of 341 acres at Maidstone in Manchester, divided it into lots of from one to fifteen acres, and sold to the ex-slaves for small amounts and, in some cases, no down-payment at all. My own ancestors benefited from such a scheme at Beaufort, and there were others across the island.

The contribution of the Moravians and other denominations to the development of Jamaica should not be undervalued. When the sceptics of today begin to question the role of the Church in our society, those who have positive recollections must record and publish them for the enlightenment of the 'Doubting Thomases'. We all must acknowledge not only where we are coming from and how much we owe to the past, but also the obligation to repay our debt to the past. This is the spirit in which I have lived and I strongly recommend it to my fellow Jamaicans seeking to make our country a better place for all.

3

On to Duke Street

My faith in God was amply rewarded from the very first day with Aunt Margaret in Kingston. She was a good woman, very kind to me; and I was aware that she was a young widow with three daughters, the youngest was Shirley, and a home she had just bought. In addition, she had to adjust to returning to Jamaica after a long stay in America. Despite all this, she gave me guidance, encouragement and motivation to face the challenges I was to encounter. It was a sad day for all of us when she returned to the United States in order to provide the income needed for her family. She left her children and me in the care of Aunt Rachel who had her own daughter Phyllis with her as well. Now there was a little bit of Parson Reid in Waltham Park Road.

In 1934, I was a resident of Kingston, no longer a visiting student. All I wanted then was a job, money to buy food, nice clothes to wear to church and a little savings to send back home. I was unaware of the seething discontent in the country and I did not know that there were men of conscience seeking ways to change the old order. However, a series of unlikely events led me into the thick of trade unionism and politics. Before too long, I would become deeply involved in the movement to reform Jamaica. The folks at home would marvel at the fact that the quiet, Sunday-school organist from Ashton was in the forefront of a national upheaval, fighting for the under-paid working class and the hungry unemployed. Almost all my working days have been spent in this service; even now, so late in life, I am still fully committed to trade unionism and I propose to continue that way until the breath has left my body.

The upward climb in Kingston was not as easy as my rural family believed. The harsh reality was that there were more dogs than bones and that the meat was being distributed according to colour and class. I was more aware of this after my experiences in Montego Bay and I began to realise that even newspaper advertisements for jobs mentioned skin colour as a qualification. It was not unusual to read in the *Gleaner:*

> *Young lady (white) with Junior Cambridge Certificate, desires position in a refined home as governess or nursing governess.*

or,

> *Respectable young man (fair) late of the country, desires position as valet or waiter.*

or,

> *Coloured girl, attractive, seeks position as nursery governess or clerk in a store.*

or,

> *Respectable coloured girl (dark) with 2 years hospital training requires position in respectable home as mother's help.*

Although I was young and inexperienced, this colour discrimination did not seem right to me. I came to realise that it must have existed in Kingston on my first stay there, but it was only when I began seriously to look for work that I began to see the implications of such advertisements and the difficulties they presented, especially to most young Jamaicans who wanted to get ahead in the world. Because I was not of light complexion I could not hold a job of any kind in a commercial bank. Though I was proficient at arithmetic and knew how to speak to people, I could not find employment selling cloth, shoes or books in any King Street store. But I was not ready to give up.

One Sunday morning when my cousins and I were on our way to service at the Church of the Redeemer, we saw a tall gentleman, well-dressed and of light complexion, standing alone at one of the intersections on Duke

Street. He had both hands in his pockets, while pensively observing the scene. As we approached, he smiled, grasped the lapels of his coat and asked, "Where are you going, little girls?"

Being the eldest, I replied, "To church over there, sir."

He chuckled, clasped his hands and said, "Please take care how you cross the street and be good little girls." With that, he walked away, hands firmly tucked in his pockets.

I was very impressed with this stranger who had taken time to speak to us. I had been told that in Kingston people were not as polite as country folk and wouldn't speak readily to strangers. More than that, white people were not supposed to have much interest in black people. So I kept wondering who was this unusual man.

I was to see him again and again, each time I walked to church. He would usually be engaged in animated conversation with some person.Sometimes I would get a wave of the hand and a smile, but more often he was too busy to see me going by. I had often wondered about the subject of his conversations with the men and women around him. I had no answer. I knew only that he lived nearby, at a boarding house named Egremont House, then at 87 Duke Street by the corner of Charles Street, and now just an open lot. Little could I know or even suspect that our chance meeting on Duke Street was to be the beginning of a new life for me – a near fifty-year relationship with Alexander Bustamante. Was that a mere coincidence, or was it the hand of God? Was it an accident that the very year of my return to Kingston as a permanent resident was also the year, 1934, that Mr Bustamante returned to Jamaica for good?

My quest for employment ended temporarily when a friend, Miss Sangster, invited me to fill her place while she took a vacation from her post at Arlington House. The job entailed work as cashier, typist and clerk at Arlington House Hotel and Restaurant. In those days, tasks were not sharply defined. A young worker did whatever was there to be done. So while I was there, I had no time for idling, little time for personal concerns and lots of opportunity to learn about business and the ways of customers and fellow workers.

Arlington House in the nineteen-thirties, was a favourite meeting place for public figures, particularly those involved in politics. It was, and still is, located at 60 East Queen Street where it was established by Mr R.W. Lindsay who, incidentally, had been a friend of Mr Bustamante when they were both in Panama. The restaurant had an interesting clientele including Elected Members of the Legislative Council and others concerned with public affairs.

In the short time that I spent at Arlington House, I was able to see and hear such political spokesmen of the day as Mr E.V.V. Allen, a pharmacist and businessman who was to be elected in 1935 as Member of the Legislative Council for St Elizabeth. Others among the diners and debaters were Felix Gordon Veitch of Hanover, Philip Lightbody of St James and Peter Sangster, an uncle of former Prime Minister Donald Sangster. Mr Bustamante also frequented the establishment to eat and to join in the lively discussions. His remark on seeing me at Arlington House was, "Oh, you are the church lady!"

I developed a keen interest in the daily after-dinner conversations which took place at Arlington House. The men would talk about the plight of the poor, the lack of public utilities, the need for jobs and better working conditions and the inadequacy of representational politics: there was only one elected Member of the Legislative Council for each parish, and the voters had to own a certain amount of land. They also spoke passionately about the vast majority of Jamaican adults being unemployed – only about 18 per cent of the people were said to have any income at all; and most of those employed were earning less than twenty-five shillings a week. The speakers felt that although they might have been elected to serve the people, they very often handled issues as independent individuals, without a common plan or strategy. They had neither administrative responsibility or any power to make laws for the benefit of those they represented.

The intensity of these debates was heightened by the fact that the elections of 1935 were soon to come and the Arlington House patrons included not only active politicians but also a good number of journalists cementing their contacts and searching for stories of interest to their readers. It was here that I first met Theodore Sealy who was to become Editor-in-Chief of the *Gleaner*, and a young enthusiastic reporter, Evon Blake. He later became publisher of *Spotlight Magazine*, renamed *Newday*; and also the pictorial book, *Beautiful Jamaica*.

In 1935 only seven per cent of the people had the registered right to vote; a constituency was an entire parish and candidates had to rely heavily on their personal popularity to win a seat. This meant getting their names into the newspapers, because there was no local radio station to carry information. Electronic loud speakers were non-existent, roads were rough, town centres few and far between and transportation slow and unreliable. My interest in all these things was excited by my admiration for Mr Bustamante who, though he held no public office and was not a candidate for anything, seemed so intensely moved whenever he spoke about the young and the deprived. I became increasingly concerned about the problems I heard being analysed in those discussions, but it was all cut short when Mr Lindsay's secretary returned. Once again I was among the unemployed.

With time on my hands and no promise of a job I turned to reading any publication that I could find, but not only in the hope of finding work. Now that I had become aware of the problems facing Jamaica, I began to read the papers more seriously and to look out for any speeches or contributions made by the men I had listened to in Arlington House.

There were powerful voices to speak for the wealthy and the socially entrenched. At that time, there were organisations and institutions of great influence, such as the Jamaica Imperial Association, actively advocating Britannia's right to rule the waves. Big planters, industrialists, and some of the merchants, as well as the appointed representatives of the colonial administration controlled the wealth, held key positions in the country and, having the voting strength which was at the time reserved for property-owners, were able to determine what was good for the island. Invariably this meant what was good for them rather than for the masses of the Jamaican people.

The men at the top were not alone in organising themselves. Their wives and others of that social bracket were quite as active and became members of groups such as the Victoria League, founded in England in 1901 and faithfully copied in Jamaica nine years later. This preceded the Jamaica Imperial Association which was founded in 1917. However, it must be acknowledged that many of these women used their unquestionable influence to good advantage and devoted themselves to important social work, particularly among needy children. It was they who got the Government to remove the orphan's home from the unsuitable Bumper Hall to what is now known as the Maxfield Park Children's Home. They also pioneered the Child Welfare Association, among other service groups.

The ladies of leisure were not the only ones to bring the benign influence of women to bear upon the ills of the Jamaican society. Women closer to the masses were setting the pace for a more general public awareness of conditions affecting the majority of the population. Several of these were educators, among them Amy Bailey whose family lived opposite Tutorial College. She was a teacher at Kingston Technical School and she it was who confronted Governor Sir Edward Denham with the request that graduates of technical schools be allowed to enter the Civil Service on equal terms with graduates from colleges and high schools. She won that battle and so opened doors of opportunity for tens of thousands of boys and girls whose standard of education had been unjustly regarded as inferior.

Young people who had been educated in private secondary schools were also subject to some discrimination and, as one of these, I had experienced my share of disappointments. By early 1936 I was growing very discouraged with my lack of success in job-hunting when I got some encouraging news from a Mrs Prestwidge who was building a house at Hagley Park Road, not far from ours on Waltham Park Road. She had lived in the United States for many years and was well acquainted with my relatives. According to Mrs Prestwidge, she had a friend named Bustamante who might be able to give me employment.

He had offices on Duke Street and was looking for someone to keep his books, take notes, type letters and run the office generally. She thought I would be able to do the job and suggested that I apply as soon as possible. I was tickled at the prospect of meeting my friend once more and quickly agreed to go and apply.

The next Monday morning, dressed in my Sunday best, I went to 1A Duke Street and was told to sit for a while. As I waited, I noticed that there was an elderly gentleman taking care of some books and a young lady who seemed uncomfortable and unfamiliar with what she was doing. Soon I was ushered into the presence of Mr Bustamante. He seemed pleasantly surprised to see me and enquired if I had left Arlington House. I told him that I had been a temporary employee and he said that whether I had left or not I could have the job if I wanted. He had observed me at Arlington House and had been impressed by my energy and devotion to duty. He was confident that I would do just fine in his office. I took the job. It was March 9, 1936, just a day after my twenty-fourth birthday.

So fate, or God, had taken another hand in my life. I was to spend the next three years as Bustamante's Girl Friday, doing all the office work, but mostly typing letters to the editors of newspapers and to various officials in and out of the island. One of these letters, addressed to Major Clement Attlee, leader of the British Labour Party, summed up the Jamaican situation with great accuracy. It said in part, 'The pot of discontent is boiling. Today it has reached the brim. Tomorrow it may overflow . . . '

I took up my new job with pride and great expectations of becoming involved more with people than with paper and pencil. Somehow, the pay, a pound a week, did not seem to matter as much as the prospect of doing something important and enjoying the prestige of working on the famous Duke Street where most of the leading barristers and solicitors had their offices. This phase of my life was yet another link in the chain of coincidence connecting me with Duke Street. First it was my church, then my school, then my initial encounter with Mr Bustamante. Now, I was at work at a Duke Street address and later I would have other work on the same street.

Mr Bustamante's attorneys, Judah and Randall, were at Number 11, Duke Street, and he had an especially close and friendly relationship with N.N. Nethersole, a lawyer and budding politician with offices at Number 3. I also became close to these Duke Street gentlemen; and when I started to save some of my wages, it was to Victoria Mutual Building Society at Number 6 that I went. I am a member to this day, when the senior executive is Karl Wright whose father was my schoolmate. I used to meet with his mother on Duke Street when she worked with Judah and Randall.

Also on Duke Street were his cousin, Norman Manley, a leading barrister of the day, J.A.G. Smith also a lawyer and an active Member of the Legislative Council at Number 7; and Allan Wynter at Number 30, where the BITU was first located. Allan was Busta's first lawyer in Jamaica and, although a strong supporter of the PNP, he was always mindful of and concerned about Bustamante's efforts on behalf of the poor. He provided space at his offices for the Union in its early days. However, since he had a preference for chamber work, he made way for lawyer Ross Livingston when the Bustamante Industrial Trade Union was formed. One of his children, Dr Sheila Wynter, was, so to speak, born and grew up with us and became as ardent in supporting the Jamaica Labour Party as in carrying out her excellent medical practice.

Some of my best friends lived on Duke Street. I remember my frequent visits to the Carvalhos at Number 88. I think they were still there when the BITU was relocated to Number 61 1/2 . Then, of course, there were the historic activities at Headquarters House and, later, Gordon House, both on Duke Street.

Mr Bustamante's offices were on lower Duke Street, at Number 1A. The business was known as Loan and Securities Company, and was conducted in two rooms, one for the boss while the other was shared by myself and an elderly gentleman who helped with clerical work.

The accommodations were modest but very busy, with people always coming in for consultation on all sorts of matters. Two solicitors, Mr McCorkell, and a Chinese lawyer occupied rooms adjacent to us. Duke Street was known as the lawyers' street. The main legal exception to the Duke Street location was the highly-regarded firm of Milholland, Ashenheim and Stone which was on Port Royal Street, but still near to Duke Street.

Lewis Ashenheim, one of the senior partners of Milholland, Ashenheim and Stone, was, among other things, a politician and a legal defender of Marcus Garvey. He also figured in more business enterprises than any other individual of his day. He was a director and, in several instances, chairman of many prominent establishments including the Gleaner Company, a position well cemented by his marriage to Estelle DeCordova, sister of the Managing Director, Michael DeCordova. The relationship was strengthened by Michael DeCordova's marriage to Lewis Ashenheim's sister Judith. This was one of the famous double-weddings of the early twentieth century.

Reference to this marriage reminds me of another giant in the legal and business world – the Hon. Noel Livingston, the Custos of Kingston. His wife was not referred to as Mrs Livingston but as Lady Cuffe, her name by a former marriage. So when the newspaper reported some function, it would say ' . . . among those present were the Hon. Noel Livingston and Lady Cuffe.' Some time later, Livingston was made a Knight and became Sir Noel Livingston. I cannot now remember how that couple was described after that, but no doubt, Lady Cuffe became Lady Livingston.

The presence of Lewis Ashenheim on the boards of so many large businesses, gave the *Gleaner* a powerful influence among advertisers. The newspaper also benefited from the connections of its editor, Herbert George DeLisser, who as Secretary of the Jamaica Imperial Association, earned from the British monarch the honour of Companion of the Most Distinguished Order of St Michael and St George. He was also the author of the first novel to be written about the Rose Hall Estate,

The White Witch of Rose Hall, the only one of his books about Jamaica that is still read today.

With these and other powerful men controlling the *Gleaner*, the business community, the wealthy and the social elite were assured of an outlet for their views and opinions. However, the poor masses had no voice to compete for a hearing. Many tried, and none harder than Marcus Garvey who had to produce his own paper to publicise his views. There were other newspapers at the time but none with the wide readership and influence of the Gleaner. When Garvey left his homeland for the last time, there was a void which had to be filled. It was Bustamante who would do this, beginning with numerous letters to the Gleaner on a variety of public issues affecting the welfare of the inarticulate and under-represented masses. I look back now with wonder and thankfulness that from the very beginning of that service until the end of his days, I was privileged to stand with Alexander Bustamante, behind him at first and beside him ever after.

On my first day at work I decided that 'Mr Bustamante' was too long a name to say every time I had to speak with him, so I called him 'Mr B.' This did not change for the next three years until most of his followers began referring to him as 'The Chief', and I did the same. Since he himself accepted this as a term of endearment, I continued to call him Chief. He in turn called me Miss Longbridge and sometimes by my first name, which he would jokingly pronounce 'Glad Ice'.

It was a good thing that I could write rapid shorthand notes, because I quickly found out that taking dictation for a letter was nothing compared to recording notes of a conversation. Before I could translate one set of notes, there would be another discussion and another lengthy letter, an urgent errand, half a dozen different chores and also a consultation to help The Chief decide whether or not a particular approach was appropriate. It was hard and exacting work, but it gave me a great understanding of living standards among the urban poor. The poverty-stricken appearance of some of those who came to the office was in sharp contrast to the well-dressed legal practitioners and their peers in downtown Kingston.

Although the main purpose of Bustamante's office was that of lending money to people in distress, he spent more time being an advocate for the oppressed, arguing their case and articulating their cause by his untiring letter-writing. Those letters covered every subject under the sun – the poor conditions under which the people lived and worked, unjust water metering, the location of a sanitarium for tuberculosis patients, unemployment, trade, agriculture, and even the conduct and behaviour of those in high places.

A very controversial matter which concerned Mr Bustamante personally was his role as a moneylender. It was a subject that would, in the years ahead, attract the attention of political opponents seeking to challenge or assail his integrity. Yet there were at the time many money-lending agencies. To the same extent that poverty was visible in Kingston in the 1930s, so did moneylending become popular.

Among the leading lenders was the Peoples Discount and Deposit Company, owned by a group of lawyers and businessmen. It lent large and small sums for periods of thirty, sixty or ninety days, and the interest was deducted from the amount borrowed before the loan cheque was written. This company did a very large business and in most cases a guarantor or two were required to join the borrower in signing the promissory note.

Other lenders included the Liguanea Discount Company that did business on a smaller scale, and the legal firm of Milholland Ashenheim and Stone, which was reputed to be the biggest. At another level there were individuals who would save from their salaries and lend money to their co-workers, charging a shilling in the pound as interest for one week. Many lenders would arrive at business places every Friday at about noon to collect or to transact new loans. Some operated from their homes, where borrowers were asked to leave some item of property as collateral.

There is no question that the practice of moneylending was sometimes abused and that many unfortunate persons lost prized possessions because of it. However, Bustamante did not squeeze anyone. In fact, I knew of many cases in which he was never repaid and at no time did he make trouble over the matter. As I write this, I am looking at a registered title for two acres of land at Industry in St Mary. It was left with us in 1936 by a man who gave it as collateral for a loan of fourteen pounds sterling, which might have been all it was worth at the time. The borrower never returned and Bustamante made no effort to find him. Nor did we ever try to convert the holding to our use. As land does not rot, it must still be there, sixty years and more after the transaction.

The criticisms levelled at Busta the moneylender didn't seem to matter to him, but I remember that on one occasion, after a newspaper had brought up the issue, he took me aside to explain. It may have been because he was conscious of my Christian background and felt that a question might have been lurking in my mind. Of course, there was no such misgiving on my part. I listened and in the end suggested that he write to the newspaper so that others might be able to share his view of the subject. It was a lengthy letter, responding to an editorial blaming the prevalent poverty and distress on the money lenders.

> It must be patent to any average thinker that since money-lending only flourishes in consequence of the lack of means in a country... it is childish to assume that the ills suffered by the community are directly attributable to the money-lender, and that to do away with him will bring the millennium with everybody happy and prosperous. Do you realize that many a man and woman in this community has been forced to go to the money-lender to raise the means to save him or herself from being sold out or imprisoned for failing to be sufficiently 'tax-minded' and to have the money . . .to satisfy the demands of the Tax Bailiff?
>
> Do you know that without the money-lenders,the dead of plenty would have to be buried as paupers, and that many more would have to be sent to prison for all kinds of fines? . . .
>
> Much has been said about money-sharks and while I agree that there are unscrupulous money lenders, all the latter are not in the same category, but are these money-lenders who charge over 100 per cent of monies, which are very often never returned to them, worse than the dry goods store that make

> a profit from 100 to 250 per cent? Are they as much danger to the community as the shark who pays his shop girls in King Street as low as nine shillings per week, and his cashier fifteen shillings? . . . The price that is paid for labour throughout this country, with some exceptions, of course, is nauseating. . . . If money-lending should be stopped what would become of certain Elected Members when they rank amongst some of the greatest money-borrowers of Jamaica?
>
> I am,
> Alexander Bustamante

In the same letter, he also looked at the causes of the poverty and made some constructive suggestions for possible solutions.

> The existing mass of poverty, hunger and raggedness amongst the middle and labouring classes is not a thing of overnight growth . . . . Up to about twenty years ago, although there was poverty and some unemployment, these conditions were not so acute. Since then, everything has tended to accentuate them –higher cost of living, increase of population and no outlet, exclusion from good agricultural lands . . . . rapid increase of taxation . . . hardly any increase of wages, increase of inferiority of quality of imported goods, coupled with severe increase of prices, decrease in the ability and interest of administrators and representatives, and capping all, increasing steadily year after year, more and yet more spending – wasteful spending – of public money, spending not based on the increase of saleable produce by the agricultural population of the island, but spending for the sake of satisfying personal and political ambitions.
>
> The remedy? What is the use of suggesting? Will anything be done by those in authority in Jamaica, and by others who can help? I fear not. The remedy for some of the ills are:- That our people be sent back to the lands – real good lands, and be given some money to make a fair start which the Government would collect over a long period of years.
>
> That local industries be established, I should say increased, for every one of us is not suitable for agriculture . . .

The Bustamante letters created quite a stir, particularly as they were written in a language and style of protest hitherto unknown in Jamaica. In contrast to others before him who had spoken and written with more than due respect for the ruling class, he demonstrated a fearlessness and audacity that resulted in consternation among officials and adoration among those he sought to represent.

Bustamante's early life in Jamaica, his work experience both at home and abroad, his wide travels abroad and his varied experiences in Panama, Spain, Cuba, and the United States made him sensitive to the cause of the working class. He was born in a thatched cottage deep in the Jamaican countryside and though his family had property, financial independence and good connections, he had, while growing up, been close to those who worked in the fields. He left Jamaica at an early age and, in his travels became a transport supervisor in Panama, served as a soldier in Spain and fought against a rebel, Abd-el-Krim, worked as a security officer in Cuba and as a dietitian in New York. He was a great social mixer as well.

Always concerned about the good management of money and business, he had saved all he could and through wise spending and eventually by, skilful playing on the New York Stock Exchange, accumulated a fair amount of money. On a number of occasions he returned to Jamaica seeking investment opportunities. At one time he actually started a dairy business supplying milk from a Molynes Road address. He was also interested in bee-keeping, but left the island before venturing into it. Years later, however, he was to keep bees as a hobby in the garden of our house on Tucker Avenue and, after his retirement from active politics, at Bellencita.

Bustamante returned to Jamaica to settle in 1934. He had changed his name from Clarke to Bustamante. Because of this, he was obliged to remain on board his ship until his sister, Louise Purcell, arrived to identify him. Once he had landed, he headed for Annotto Bay where his mother lived, and began looking around for investment opportunities. He saw nothing to excite his interest in business but, as he said to me, "I saw that something was radically wrong with the way the poor men, women and children were living. Few had shoes on their feet, their clothes were ragged and they seemed hungry."

Going back to Kingston, he sought and received advice and assistance from the legal firm of Judah and Randall, which made investments on his behalf. It was then that he got into the money-lending business and was in closer contact with the poor and those others struggling to keep their heads above water. Because his business flourished, he was able to employ me; yet, as fate would have it, his attention turned more and more to public problems than to private concerns. Instead of being just a stenographer, doing clerical work and helping to write a volume of letters to the press, I became heavily involved with talking to the scores of troubled persons who came to 1A Duke Street with their difficulties. The talkshows of the nineties are reminiscent of the way we had to deal with pleas and complaints from the public. Most were about personal difficulties arising from the bad economic conditions, but there were others who spoke for groups concerned with broad questions involving government policies. No one was ever turned away and the numbers kept growing.

4

The Hardships of the Time

THE TURBULENT EVENTS OF 1938 were not preceded by any noticeable calm. Indeed, the period leading up to them was as thunder rolling before a heavy downpour. To many observers, the turning point in Jamaica's modern political movement came with a sudden rush out of the 1938 labour disturbances on the sugar estates and the waterfront. In fact, it was the culmination of similar outbreaks in other West Indian territories, the result of decades of social neglect and poor economic policies. Added to these were the worldwide economic depression of the thirties, the influence of the teachings of Marcus Garvey and the demands of men who had served in the West India Regiment in World War I. They had seen life outside the Caribbean and knew that the time for change was long overdue.

The warning signs of the 1930s were there for all to see and yet the colonial powers paid little heed. In 1934 there were hunger marches in Trinidad and these led to strikes among oilfield workers. Then in January 1935 sugar workers in St Kitts adamantly demanded higher wages. The response of the authorities was to summon a warship, precipitating a disturbance which left three dead and eight wounded.

Later in the year there was an uprising in St Vincent. A state of emergency was declared and again a warship summoned to help quell the rebellion. Next it was St Lucia where a strike was suppressed by soldiers, marines and the appearance of the usual warship. In 1935, Uriah 'Buzz' Butler organised a hunger march in Trinidad and the following year launched the British Empire Workers and Home Rule Party. His activities led to a strike of labourers on the forest reserves. Later, when fire broke out in the oilfields, troops from the HMS *Ajax* were brought in and Butler was thrown into prison. The trouble spread to Tobago and within weeks Barbados also was in turmoil. Clement Payne, a leader of the workers, was deported from the country on the grounds that he was born in Trinidad. This so enraged his supporters that a riot ensued, resulting in fourteen deaths and fifty-nine persons wounded. In 1935, Guyanese workers called a strike that lasted for three months.

In Jamaica also there were upheavals of unrest, quickly and severely suppressed. In May, 1935, in the face of rising unemployment, banana workers in Oracabessa, St Mary, protested violently against the introduction of workers from Port Maria. Shortly afterwards, one man died in a similar outburst among waterfront workers in Falmouth. From that point onward, there were numerous mini-strikes and other demonstrations of discontent.

The following extract from a document which we at the BITU prepared on the thirtieth anniversary of the Union gives a broader picture of the developing situation.

> Nineteen thirty-eight marked one hundred years since the abolition of slavery in Jamaica. But the mass of Jamaica's population had little to celebrate. Indeed, the conditions prevailing in the island were not far removed from the conditions of 1838.
>
> As had been the case a century before, the mainstay of Jamaica's economy, the sugar industry, was undergoing great difficulties. During World War I, the overseas price of Jamaica's sugar had risen considerably. However, with the coming of peace in 1919, prices began to fall rapidly due to an over-supply of sugar on the world market. The banana trade was also experiencing hard times. Although the industry had begun to recover at the end of the war when shipping had again become possible, it was dealt a fatal blow by Leaf Spot Disease.
>
> The effects of the low sugar price and the slump in the banana trade were felt throughout the society, but the labouring sector suffered most. Low wages, unemployment and poor working conditions were widespread. The typical wage rate for estate work (on which the majority depended) varied between sixpence and two shillings daily. For task work a man might receive between nine-pence and one shilling for clearing a square chain of land, depending on whether the surface was wooded or cultivated. If he cut a similar area of cane, he would earn between ninepence and two shillings. Women earned even less.

> Generally, the labourer did not know beforehand what he would be paid. The wage was set up by the Busha or the Overseer. But what could the labourer do about it? There were hundreds of unemployed ready and willing to take his place, so he had either to accept what he could get, or starve. . .
>
> Thousands of unemployed drifted to the city of Kingston, lured by the belief that there was work and high wages to be found on the docks. Every announcement that the Colonial Government had voted sums for public works attracted the rural unemployed. They poured into the city on cane wagons, drays, coal carts and on foot. These rural job-seekers congregated in the already unhealthy slums of Trench Pen, Kingston Pen and Dungle Hill. . . . It was estimated that in 1938, there were between ten and twelve thousand unemployed in the city of Kingston. The cost of living was high. . . . A small room cost between three and six shillings per week and, to save expenses, five or six persons would 'cotch' in a room. People crowded into these dismal, ill-ventilated tenements which lacked proper sanitary provisions. Throughout the island, health conditions were poor – tuberculosis, yaws, venereal disease, hookworm and malnutrition were rife. The illiteracy rate was high, for poverty and ill-health combined to keep school attendance low, even where accommodation was possible.
>
> In short, there was total neglect of the masses. The Colonial Government was more interested in balancing the colonyies budget. The Legislative Council reflected the structure of the society. Most of the elected members were too far removed from the masses of the people to have any real understanding of the social and economic conditions under which they existed. In fact, the bulk of the population was unrepresented, in that the views of the people's representatives were not the views of the people. . . The right to vote was based on economic position.
>
> The social structure of the island had changed little since 1838. The white minority had grown less in numbers, and much poorer, but the more important institutions and positions in the society were still under its control. The middle class had become larger, and now included a sprinkling of dark-skinned businessmen and professionals. Both sectors were equally cut off from the working class; and it was upon this latter group that the hardships of the time fell most severely.

The sudden upsurge of 1938 was not the people's only response to these conditions. That response had been simmering from as early as 1909 when Sandy Cox, the lawyer who represented St Thomas in the Legislative Council, led the National Club which expressed the belief that self- government for Jamaica was the answer. The Club's policy allowed only persons born in Jamaica to become members. It did not seek to address the specific problems of the poor but it did reflect the dissatisfaction that arose from those conditions. Twenty years later, Marcus Garvey added another stimulus to the vision by forming the People's Political Party which combined the cries for liberation from poverty with those for freedom from colonial domination. The same BITU document shows that other groups, including even the Chamber of Commerce, were struggling to make their voices heard by the Colonial Office in Westminster.

> Towards the end of the 1930s there was evidence that a new consciousness was developing within the society. In 1937 expressions of discontent issued from the vocal elements of the community and were focused in the urban areas. Citizens Associations multiplied in their number and activity and began to display considerable interest in political affairs to the extent that one association sponsored a candidate in the 1937 Corporation elections. A vigorous campaign was waged against colour prejudice and the policy of employing white expatriates in key positions which could have been filled by qualified Jamaicans.
>
> Groups such as the National Reform Association fought against political disabilities and demanded constitutional change which would allow the native population an effective part in governing the country. The Chamber of Commerce was active in protesting high customs duties and resisted the imposition of further taxation or other measures which it was thought would hamper the progress of the business sector. The Imperial Association directed its attention toward increasing Jamaica's sugar quota and Imperial Protection. Shop assistants formed an active Clerk's Association in an attempt to gain better working conditions and fair wages. All these energies went into the pot of discontent.

The most articulate call for organising the growing national spirit came from Jamaicans living overseas. It happened first in New York where, in 1936, a group led by Walter Adolphe Roberts, W.G. McFarlane and Wilfred Domingo founded the Jamaica Progressive League. In the following year, some of them came to Kingston and launched a branch of the League at a meeting held at my church – the Moravian Church of the Redeemer at North and Duke Streets.

The Jamaica Progressive League's main objective was self-government for Jamaica. That was a long-term task which would be difficult to accomplish, working from abroad. However, an incident in 1936, involving a 'returning resident', Osmond Fairclough, gave rise to another wave of activity for political change. 'O.T.' as he was often known, was a black Jamaican who had gone to Haiti and had worked as a senior accountant in a bank in Port au Prince. He returned to Jamaica in 1936 and applied to the local banks for employment. The response to all his applications was that the only jobs available were those of messenger or porter.

Stung by the rejection, which was based solely on the colour of his skin, Fairclough made a commitment to do whatever he could to bring about Jamaican self-rule. First, he started a weekly newspaper to educate Jamaicans about their right to master their own affairs. The paper, *Public Opinion*, was launched in February 1937 and, small though it was in size and circulation, it began immediately to give expression to the causes of the seething discontent and to make an impact on the middle class.

Undeterred by the fact that he had very little money, 'Fair-C.', another of his nick-names, sought support for his ideas and found it in some unexpected quarters. For instance, the first printing of the newspaper was paid for by Ansell Hart, a leading solicitor, accepted in the community as a white man. He was assisted in its publication by an Englishman, H.P. Jacobs, and a Jamaican journalist, Frank Hill. Articles were written by the intellectuals and thinkers of the day, including Philip Sherlock, Alderman William Seivright and Amy Bailey.

Public Opinion also gave opportunity to poets and other writers whose works might not have been accepted by other publications because they expressed a new level of thinking. Vivian Virtue's stirring poem 'Revolt', was typical of the rebellious spirit of the times – the young at heart questioning the subservience to the old order and vowing a change of attitudes.

Others too wrote with feeling, but none more lucidly about the desperation and the determination of the masses than the young George Campbell. He was a reporter for the *Daily Gleaner*, covering the old Resident Magistrates Court, then held in the gracious building – now a national monument – close to the St Andrew Parish Church at Half Way Tree. One of his pieces published by Public Opinion was titled 'Negro Aroused', inspired as it was by Edna Manley's well-known sculpture of the same name.

There were also other movements concerned with the general welfare of the people at the grassroots. Without a doubt, the most important of these initiatives was the launching of Jamaica Welfare Limited in 1937. Norman Manley had appealed to the United Fruit Company to fund an organisation committed to helping rural Jamaicans, in particular, to improve their standard of living through various forms of cooperative effort.

Mr Manley had proposed to the head of the company, Samuel Zemurray, that a cess be placed on bananas exported from the island; and Zemurray, not forgetting the poverty of his own youth, agreed to set aside one penny for each count-bunch of bananas for the purposes outlined to him. The cess produced a substantial sum, about twenty thousand pounds, which provided capital and working expenses for Jamaica Welfare.

In 1912 Leila James had been the first girl to win the Jamaica Scholarship. Born in Kingston,she had attended Wolmer's High School for Girls and later Bedford College in London. She had been an educationist and welfare worker in Jamaica, Costa Rica and Bermuda; had studied recreation and community projects in New York, West African dialect in Nigeria and Negro Education at Columbia University. 'Mrs T.', as she became known as, turned out to be one of the most accomplished social service workers ever in Jamaica.

This distinguished woman had once been the central figure in a heated controversy spurred by J.A.G.Smith in the Legislative Council.

The row stemmed from the fact that Leila James, upon returning to Jamaica with a B.A. degree from Oxford University, had been appointed to a senior position in the Department of Education. Never had a back woman been given such a job and, soon after, the authorities had a change of heart and transferred her to a less conspicuous office. Still, her qualifications and her capabilities kept getting in the way and after a number of shifts from post to post, she was dismissed from the service. When Smith discovered the facts of the case, he protested vigorously and called on the Governor to set up a Commission of Enquiry into the matter. After a heated exchange, the authorities agreed to the Enquiry which decided in Miss James's favour and ordered her reinstatement.

Other outstanding workers in the forefront of the early Welfare movement were Evan Donaldson, D.T.M. Girvan and Eddie Burke. Some were sent to the University of Antigonish in Nova Scotia and some to England to study the work of the Rochdale Pioneers in developing cooperatives. Upon their return and their venture out into the field, some parts of Jamaica began to be aware of and to set up for the first time institutions such as credit unions and to organise themselves into cooperatives for a variety of purposes.

The manner in which the credit union meetings were structured in the early years tended to bring people of different social groupings together. The meetings were convened under trees, in church halls, school yards, in the homes of members or wherever was convenient for the interested parties. Meetings would begin with the singing of folk songs, followed by discussions concerning the needs of the community and how they might be met by cooperative action. At the end, members would pay up their shillings and sixpences, but not before studying Tom Girvan's booklet, *Let's Study and Save Together*. After regular study of Parts 1 and 2 of that booklet, the groups would turn to another of Girvan's texts, *Let's Study and Work Together*. This would lead to cooperative action in housing and consumer projects, including shops where individual members would buy goods they acquired by the group at wholesale rates.

Then came the community centres established by Jamaica Welfare. Whenever one of these was being opened at places such as Porus, Guy's Hill, or Frankfield, Manley would stress the point that the place was for everyone and that Jamaicans should recognise one another as brothers and sisters working together for the common good. It was the type of thinking and exhortation that was filtering through the country in 1937. Yet there was resistance to these innovations intended to improve the lot of the rural worker. The social awareness of some would be awakened only by the violent working-class reaction that was to come. The times were changing and the dominant mood was one of anger and frustration. Once again, I quote from the BITU document which here clearly identifies the different sections of society which were adversely affected by the circumstances of the time:

> The year 1937 saw a spate of public meetings and resolutions were passed urging the Colonial Government to improve conditions. Letters published in the daily newspapers asserted that the middle class had been reduced to a state of 'decent pauperism' as it was impossible to maintain the standard of living . . . Throughout the year there were several strikes and demonstrations to draw attention to the plight of the masses. Each month brought a new wave of unrest from scattered parts of the island. The idea of trade unionism had not yet gained the notice or support of the working class and the one or two unions that existed were weak and ineffectual.
>
> Hunger marches were a popular way of expressing discontent. The ex-servicemen of the British West India Regiment who had served in the Great War of 1914 had returned home to join the ranks of the unemployed. They founded an Association which organised deputations to the Governor and Colonial Secretary, but without tangible result. In August 1937, the Association planned to march to King's House in another effort to invite some action on their behalf. Armed with banners and placards which illustrated their demand for 'land or work', the group assembled at the Kingston Race Course as their starting point.
>
> The police were quickly on the scene and closed the exits from the grounds, thus defeating the attempts of the ex-soldiers to move out on to the streets. The Colonial Secretary arrived and addressed the gather-

> ing and exhorted the crowd to ". . . have faith in His Excellency, as there is only one person who can give you what you want, and that is the Governor." But the men showed that they were no longer content to accept the smooth promises of the administration. A section of the crowd attempted to defy the police barriers and were suppressed with blank shots and batons. Several persons were injured in the clash. Public panic was soothed by a report that the incident had been caused by the 'hooligan element' and was one that ' . . . nobody in his right senses would regard as serious.'
>
> During March, about 60 per cent of the labour force went on strike for higher wages at the Gray's Inn Sugar Factory. The crop was reaped by the other 40 per cent who had to work under police supervision. Banana cutters and carriers in different parts of the island staged several strikes, none of which lasted for any appreciable time because of the quick action of the police and the threats of employers. On one occasion strikers were faced with the alternative of 24 hours notice of dismissal or an immediate return to work. On another property, those strikers occupying estate barracks were given notice of eviction. In each case they went back to work without delay. When they had grievances and requested audience with their employers, they were often met with flat refusal, and even when a hearing was granted, they returned to their jobs as soon as their story had been told.
>
> In a situation in which unemployment was widespread there was no shortage of strike-breakers. There was as yet no sense of identity between those who were protesting against poor working conditions and those who had no work at all. The strikers were sometimes appeased with the addition of a few pence to their wages, but these cases were rare. Therefore, despite the new militancy of the working classes, the gains were few. They lacked organization. They lacked unity. They lacked leadership.

During the early part of 1937, Bustamante attended several meetings arranged by citizens association, which, at that time, were the main political organizations. The first at which he spoke was in Smith Village, now known as Denham Town, in Western Kingston. He also gave speeches before gatherings of the Social Reconstruction League and at each of these he would denounce the social and economic conditions as well as the institutions and individuals he thought responsible for maintaining the status quo. He also made it his business to visit public meetings in an effort to assess the readiness of the people for the struggles that he felt most certainly lay ahead.

Public meetings were common in Kingston during those turbulent days. Speakers had only makeshift platforms, no electric lights and no microphones. They had to throw their voices with volume and passion; and their subject had to be of burning interest in order for them to get a hearing and to hold the crowd. One of the leaders of these street corner meetings was St William Grant, a former portworker who, during World War I, had stowed away to England to join the West India Regiment. After returning to Jamaica, he went to New York and there became a member of the militant Tiger Division of Marcus Garvey's UNIA in New York.

Grant returned to Jamaica in 1934 as a delegate to the UNIA's International Convention. However, his style of speaking and his explosive temper soon put him in trouble with Garvey who told him to leave the movement. He did not go back to America, but stayed in Jamaica and continued to carry the message with fearless speech and tireless action. In addition to the Back-to-Africa theme, he also turned his attention to the more urgent issues of wages, working conditions, cost of living and unemployment. Dressed in a military-style uniform and bearing the flag of Garvey, he was easily the most colourful of the street corner orators of the time. His audiences were large and enthusiastic.

St William's main stomping ground was Victoria Park, which was to be named after him during the 1980s. He also held meetings at North Parade, at Coke Chapel steps and along the Spanish Town Road. One night I went with Bustamante to a meeting being held by Grant. In the middle of his harangue, he saw Bustamante in the crowd and pointed him out as a champion of the people's cause. He invited him to speak to the audience and when one man raised objections because of Busta's colour, Grant angrily confronted the dissident and might have attacked him had not Busta intervened.

That night Bustamante spoke of the many ills he had observed since his return to Jamaica; and he pledged that he would dedicate the rest of his life to the fight to bring about a change for the better among the working class. The people cheered and, in the end, Grant told them that he was prepared to join forces with Bustamante, even as he had joined with Garvey in defying the might of the opposition. It was at that point that an unwritten alliance was formed between the two. After the meeting, Busta told me that Grant's unqualified expressions of confidence have given him further strength to fight for the people.

After that episode, we began to travel extensively to different parts of the island in search of first-hand information and eye-witness accounts of the conditions under which the poor and disenfranchised had to live. We had meetings at street corners, in bars and on piazzas, in village shacks, at farm gates and wherever the proverbial two or three might gather to express their grievances, their hopes and aspirations. Here again we found that the major worries of the people were about bread and butter issues. Nonetheless, we always took the opportunity to advise them that many of their problems arose because the laws of the land and the policies of the government were not designed for their benefit. Bustamante would address the crowd in a loud, carrying voice, since there were no microphones, while I and others with us would mingle with the people to hear from those who came to listen and were willing to talk but didn't feel like speaking up in a public way.

As word began to spread about our successful meetings, we received more and more requests for speaking engagements. In addition, Bustamante got an invitation from Mr A.G.S. Coombs, who wanted him to become associated with the Jamaica Workers and Tradesmen Union which he had founded in May 1936. Coombs was a former policeman and, like St William Grant, he had served in the West India Regiment. He too had been inspired by the teachings of Marcus Garvey and had become a supporter of St William Grant. His new union had attracted more support than most others of its kind and was spreading from Kingston to St Catherine, St Mary and St James. However, as is the case with many poor people's movements, there was more enthusiasm than money, and Coombs was obliged to support the Union from his own earnings as a road contractor with the Public Works Department.

The need for financial support must have been one of the main causes for Coombs's invitation to Bustamante. In fact, he himself wrote a public letter some time afterwards, saying that he had heard of Busta's wealth and generosity as well as his great interest in assisting the workers. Whatever the motive, Coombs had no difficulty in persuading Bustamante to speak on his platform as it provided a further opportunity for meeting the people. Before long, Busta accepted the offer which Coombs had made for him to become an officer of the Union.

From the outset, Busta made it clear that the workers' money should be protected at all costs and that he would not wish to be a part of any organisation that did not give full accounting for the handling of dues. He said he would support the Union only if he could keep a close eye on its financial operations. Coombs agreed and Bustamante was asked to take over the post of Treasurer.

Things began to happen fast and furiously as soon as Bustamante officially joined the JWTU Executive. In September 1937, we travelled to Montego Bay where a few years before I had noticed the awful conditions affecting banana workers. Now they were beginning to protest and so I gladly accompanied Bustamante, Coombs and Leslie Washington Rose to the meeting there. Rose, a strong supporter of Marcus Garvey, was also organiser for the JWTU in Spanish Town. The crowd greeted every speaker with wild enthusiasm, but it was Bustamante who mesmerised them with fearless statements against the government and certain of the employer class. His reputation as a fearless writer and speaker had preceded him and the audience cheered wildly as he spoke against the sins of the establishment. By the time the meeting was over, it was clear that Busta and not Coombs was the man in charge.

It soon became obvious that Bustamante's presence in the Union was the drawing card for large numbers of new members who felt that he was the best man to represent their case. He was happy with that development, but told me of his concern about the weaknesses of the Union's administration. As Treasurer, he had a responsibility to ensure that every penny was accounted for, but there were others who seemed not to share his views. He kept complaining and when he could get no satisfactory result, he called me take dictation of his letter of resignation.

Elsewhere it has been published that Bustamante was expelled from the JWTA after he had accepted its Presidency from Coombs in October 1937. There may have been an offer but, as far as I know, it was never accepted and could hardly have been so when Busta's resignation as Treasurer, typed by me and addressed to Coombs, was dated October 5, 1937. He also sent another letter, dated October 15, to the JWTU Executive confirming his severance from the Union. It has also been reported that the supposed expulsion was engineered by the Secretary, Hugh Buchanan, who had strongly objected to a moneylender being associated with or leading a trade union. I do not know how this can be reconciled with the fact that Buchanan was a member of the Executive that unanimously accepted Busta into the JWTA and also the first person to serve as Secretary of the Bustamante Industrial Trade Union when it was founded in 1938.

The following extracts from Bustamante's letter of 5 October 1937 to Coombs should set the record straight.

> Mr. A.G.S. Coombs,
> President,
> Jamaica Workers & Tradesmen Union,
> 141 King Street,
> Kingston
>
> Dear Sir:
>
> I must now tender my resignation as Treasurer for the Jamaica Workers and Tradesmen Union for which I was unanimously appointed by the Executive body that was present at the recent Executive Meeting. I do not intend going into much detail. However, I have reasons to feel that the financial part will not run as smoothly as it should; and as my honour is above everything else, I have decided to withdraw. I am not satisfied with the very first and only financial statement you sent me. There are times when vouchers for miscellaneous expenses cannot be obtained, but when expense runs into the sum of

£38.19.1 1/2 and no vouchers are sent to substantiate even a part, I would not with any sincerity approve of them, however true they may be, as they can only be proven from a legal standpoint by vouchers.

Five pounds (£5) were sent from Montego Bay many days ago as their first amount re purchasing the car. Although that money should have been turned over to me, up to now I have no knowledge that you have even received it. I do not care if you used it for something else than that for which it was intended, but the matter should immediately be communicated with this office, and as a matter of fact, it could not be justly used for anything but the intended purpose.

Everybody who works for the organisation must be paid; Mr. Rose and your salary should not be rated according to your former earning, but should be paid according to the position you hold. The Executive Committee must be intelligent enough to realise that this is the correct way. You should be fairly well paid, the positions call for it.

There is nothing about you that I dislike and I am sure that I could help to make that organisation a very successful one. However, I have decided to sever all and every connection with it. From what was stated by some of the officers in the recent members meeting at Spanish Town where I attended, there is not the slightest doubt that deception was used in enrolling members. That is the reason why the people were so angry over there at a previous meeting which you attended and which broke up in disorder. Deception at no time should be used in any business, for when it is found out it brings suspicion upon the leaders, and even if it were not found out, should never be done. The only way to start an organisation is on the naked truth of the views and aims, and no bait should be thrown out whether it was intended for good or bad. It was even stated publicly by officers of that said branch that you borrowed either five or six pounds to return it. I suppose that this money was to carry on other Union work, nevertheless the mere fact that they said that it was promised to be returned and they have heard nothing since then, is sufficient reason for suspicion and reflections. Most of the grievances of the Spanish Town section were apparently based on deception of some kind.

I will not associate myself with deception of any kind and I will not help anyone to prove that deception is not deception. I am far from being perfect, but in all my transactions I endeavour to be absolutely straightforward so as to get the respect of even my enemies (if any). One must be more careful with a public organisation than even his own private business, because in a public organisation it is the membership that counts most, not just a few leaders, for generals cannot conquer without soldiers . . .

Heretofore in Jamaica, organisations were formed with a pretence to help the masses, which eventually had proven not to have been so. The people therefore have become very suspicious, and rightly so; those who did not steal, I understand, wasted funds, sold out the people as soon as they got jobs, etc. One can easily see, therefore, why everything should be done to give this organisation much more prestige so as to eradicate out of their minds, but so much jealousy, narrow-mindedness and unprogressive thinking exist in this Union Headquarters that just to satisfy their own whims and fancies they would rather not do that. Leaders are to forget themselves completely and think of the members and do everything that is possible to instill in them confidence; otherwise, instead of growing it will smash.

In your presence in my office, your General Secretary openly stated that he would not want to have anybody of outstanding character and personality at the extreme head of the organisation, as he would become an idol, loved more than the others; and the other leaders would be forgotten; that it is his duty to teach the members not to think any more of one of the leaders than of the others. God gives every man his own personality and ability; he endowed some with something which others have not got, and yet your general secretary thinks he can teach the members to have the same confidence in all men. Your brother who is another adviser, fully agreed with the opinion of the General Secretary; you, being President, who should know better, and should have more ability than they, manifested that you fully understood what they meant. I do not want to hurt, but surely one hundred thousand workers at least are entitled to more progressive thinking, less selfishness, jealousy and narrow-mindedness; they are entitled to the best business ability that can be obtained, for leaders have not alone to think of the destiny of the workers of today, but of tomorrow and after . . .

With regards to the constitution, this is not one to be proud of; it is contradictory . . . instead of getting a respectable lawyer of a firm or a firm of lawyers with some standing in the community to draw the amendment, it is left in the hands of a General Secretary. This is unfair to the members because there should be no doubts as to their rights and also to the officers' . . . . Shrewd businessmen realise it is better to get a £50 per week executive than to get a £2 per week one, for what counts is results and not cheapness. The document should be made by a lawyer and paid for.

Severing my connection with this Union does not mean the divorcing of my interest in the workers. I shall do everything to see that they are lifted out of the gutter; there shall be no deception and there will be no suspicion concerning their money, for they will be told the truth from the start. I am sorry to sever my connections with your Divisional Secretaries; there are some above the average intelligence, with business understanding whilst others possess common sense; and you Mr. President, I am sorry to leave you for I know I could be of great use to you and the organisation . . . If I were looking a job in the Union to make a living then I would hang on . . .

Certain remarks made by your General Secretary in my office when he

> referred to Marcus Garvey are nothing but bold effrontery . . . and when he made a slurring remark against Captain Cipriani, an outstanding Labour Leader, then I wonder how such a person will be able to help to carve out the destiny of so many people when he talks without knowledge. Perhaps he would like to go to Trinidad and instill in the hearts of the people that which he said is his bound duty to instill in those of Jamaica, not to love and follow any outstanding labour leader because that is bad for the organisation. He needs sympathy, and you, Mr. President, if you continue understanding what he means, very soon you will need more sympathy yourself, and that's that.
>
> I must now call on you for a proper and final financial statement, and as soon as I have received this and have looked through it, I shall have much pleasure in returning to you the Union bank book.
>
> Yours faithfully
> A. Bustamante

The letter to the JWTU Executive followed the same line

The argument between Coombs and Bustamante went on for months. Norman Manley and Sir Walter Citrine of the British Trades Union Council and a member of the Royal Commission appointed after the upheavals of 1938 tried in vain for reconciliation as late as December of that year. However, both Bustamante and Coombs went on to make their contribution to Jamaica's development, each in the context of his opportunity to serve and his ability to work with the people and the organisations involved.

True to his word, Bustamante remained firmly committed to the workers' movement even after his disappointing experience in the JWTU. He did not let up one bit. If anything,, his enthusiasm escalated and my work, as well as his, increased with each report of unrest in the country – and there were many. Sporadic work stoppages were taking place on the banana plantations and cane fields around the island. Waterfront workers were continuing to show resentment and just about everywhere labourers were expressing discontent. But it was not only 'blue collar' workers who were restive. Workers in the service sector seemed to be catching the mood.

Protests began to come from hotel workers through their newly formed Jamaica Hotel Employees Association and, in the last few months of 1937, clerks in the dry goods stores in Kingston were clamouring for shorter working hours and improvement in their wages and working conditions. They threatened to shut down the stores during the busy Christmas shopping season and might have done so, but for negotiations by the Clerks' Union. Peace was restored when the store owners responded favourably and the Government quickly passed a Shop Assistants Law, allowing for limited hours of work and a half-day break each week.

The Clerks' Union was formed in 1937 by a distinguished Jamaican, popularly known and referred to by his full name, Ethelred Erasmus Adolphus Campbell. Its principal organiser was a young accountant who also liked to use his full name, Florizel Augustus Glasspole. He eventually became the third Governor General of Jamaica. Another associate, who served as vice-president of the Union, was Ernest Rae who had played cricket for the West Indies in 1936 and won a seat in the KSAC Council in 1937.

Bustamante's towering presence in that period has certainly dimmed the contribution made by some other leaders. But Jamaica should never forget people like Erasmus Campbell who rose from humble origins to become an outstanding barrister, a chemist, a politician and trade unionist and a Member of the Legislative Council for the Parish of Kingston. As a young man, he left Jamaica with an elementary school education, to work in Panama. He then went on to the United States to enter the famous Tuskagee Institute of which Booker T. Washington was once the principal. After attending other schools in America, he returned to Jamaica as a government-employed industrial research chemist and was responsible for extracting oil from pimento leaves; and also made vanillin.

A small but very self-confident individual, Campbell felt frustrated by the lack of recognition for his work. He decided to study law, one of the prestige professions of the time. He went to McGill University in Canada and Edinburgh University in Scotland before being called to the Bar in 1929, the year he was also admitted to practice in Jamaica. His own hard work and self-sacrifice had given him a feeling for the suffering of the underdog. This led to his founding of the Clerks' Union after observing the conditions under which women were working in the stores. They were earning only ten shillings weekly for unspecified hours of work, generally between 9 a.m. and 4 p.m. on weekdays and between 9 a.m. and 8 p.m. on Saturdays. During the Christmas season, they would toil, without rest, up to 11 at night. It was the Clerks' Union that got them some relief, including the half-day break which persists to this time.

Recollections of the advent of white-collar workers and professionals into the trade union movement stir up memories of the class distinctions which pervaded Jamaican society, particularly during the first half of the twentieth century. For instance, one of the first unions to be formed in the island was the Jamaica Union of Teachers, founded in 1895 by the famous Bailey family, once popularly referred to as 'The Royal Family of Teachers in Jamaica'. That union is still flourishing in Jamaica today under the name of the Jamaica Teachers Association, which it took on after amalgamating with other teachers' organisations.

It is true that such things as wage increases were not among the original objectives of the JUT. It sought to obtain benefits from the collective experience of teachers on matters to do with education; to improve the qualifications and status of teachers, to help them find employment and to advocate legislation concerning popular education. In order to further these causes, it eventually affiliated with the National Union of Teachers of Great Britain and also the Caribbean Union of Teachers. However, in the 1930s, when the trade union movement began to grow strong in other parts of the Caribbean, the JUT objected to being referred to as a trade union. A history of the JUT, published at the time, stoutly rejected the term 'trade union'; and accordingly, the organisation kept its distance from the hurly burly of that turbulent decade.

Looking back over the first two years that I worked with Bustamante, I can see how in 1936 and 1937 he seemed to find his mission in life: to improve the quality of life for the poor and to be a voice for those who had no one to speak for them. First came the letters to the press which aroused interest in all sections of the country. He called on Members of the Legislative Council to wake up from their slumber and do something for the poor people of the country besides talking. The poor themselves began to feel that they had someone who had their interests at heart. Then he began to travel all across the country by car and I went with him, often as the driver. We went to remote little districts, speaking to the people, seeing how they lived and noting their problems, which were very much the same wherever we went. The chief problems were the bad roads, or no roads at all, which meant that farmers could not carry their produce out to market and children going to school faced all kinds of difficulty; lack of a clean, reliable supply of water; generally appalling conditions and everywhere unemployment. These were the conditions that Bustamante exposed in his letters.

I also made regular visits with Mr B. to the wharves, including the Royal Mail Wharf, and saw how hard the port workers had to labour. He spoke to them from time time, spoke to the wharfinger who was a Mr Pixley, father of the Frank Pixley, attorney-at-law and later Parliamentarian, and grandfather of the late Dick Pixley, a famous radio personality. Mr Pixley told us that he was quite sympathetic, but he could do nothing about the system since the officials made the decisions. Bustamante also complained bitterly about the working conditions of the port workers and I have no doubt that his letters championing the cause of the rural labourers and the port workers helped to trigger the upheavals that were to come across the island and especially at Serge Island in St Thomas, Frome in Westmoreland and on the Kingston waterfront.

5

Nineteen Thirty-eight

CHRISTMAS 1937 PASSED WITHOUT the celebrations being marred by anxieties about unrest, particularly since the strike of store clerks had been averted. The traditional things had been done to mark the coming of 1938 – the usual Watch Night Services, the beating drums of the Jonkunoo bands prancing in the streets next day; church services again on Sunday morning and the customary tramcar ride to Hope Gardens in the afternoon.

Monday, January 3 was the first working day of 1938 and on Tuesday hundreds of workers went on strike for better wages at Serge Island sugar estate in St Thomas. This property, known commercially as the Seaforth Sugar & Rum Co. Limited, was owned by the influential Rudolf Ehrenstein, a wealthy businessman, representative of the Imperial Association and Member of the Legislative Council for the parish. Incidentally, he had been born in Czechoslovakia and in 1945 changed his family name to Elder.

The workers on strike picketed offices, blocked roads and halted cane carts. When the police broke up the crowd, angry workers armed themselves with machetes, sticks and stones and moved from house to house menacing officials and the clerical staff.

When news of the strike reached us in Kingston, Bustamante and I decided to go to the scene and to act on behalf of the workers in trying to settle the dispute. By the time we got there on the Wednesday, the roadblocks which had been mounted the previous day had been cleared and the police had dispersed the strikers. At first the strikers greeted us with suspicion, but Bustamante soon won a measure of confidence from the gathering when he said, in his charismatic style that he was prepared to speak fearlessly on their behalf, even as he had done for others in the newspapers and on street corners. The workers listened and then told us that they wanted two shillings a ton instead of the tenpence halfpenny they were getting.

We were told that Mr Ehrenstein was at his office in Morant Bay, at the Hope & Co. wharf. Mr B. said, "I'll go and see him right away," and we left Seaforth and drove to Morant Bay.

Mr Ehrenstein treated us with courtesy and was easy to talk to and understand, in spite of his European accent. This was the first time that Mr B. was dealing directly with an employer in a labour dispute. Ehrenstein told us that the estate was still recovering from trade difficulties and said that, in the interest of all, it would be best to keep wage claims at a moderate level until the situation improved. The discussion went back and forth, with the Seaforth overseers also making their contribution.

Being a reasonable man and wanting to avert the possibility of a lengthy and perhaps bloody struggle, Mr B. thought that it would be better to advise the strikers to accept the offer of one shilling a ton for the time being. This would mean less hardship for the workers and their families and would allow time for further negotiations in a more tranquil atmosphere.

However, the workers were not satisfied with the offer, nor would they hear our proposals. They felt that the management would not be persuaded by talk and that the only way to win was by violent means.They resumed their demonstration which resulted in a clash with the local police strengthened by reinforcements from Kingston. Thirty-four strikers were injured and sixty of them charged with rioting and other offences. Later, some of those who went to court were imprisoned or fined. As everything calmed down, the demonstrators all went back to work, grudgingly accepting the interim shilling a ton that had been proposed.

Serge Island was a victory that Busta did not savour, nor did I, for we both felt that much of the hurt and bitterness could have been avoided if the workers had not been pressed to the point of being unreasonable. At one point I noticed that he seemed a little disconsolate and, thinking that it might have been caused by the earlier rejection of his recommendation to the strikers, I told him that it was a great beginning and that as we went along we would not always get everything we wanted for the workers. It was then that he revealed what was really bothering him. He told me how much he disliked physical violence. He had experienced it more than once when he was abroad and had witnessed the suffering it caused to innocent people. From this time on, he decided he would always advise workers to make violence an act of last resort. He was willing to die for the cause of the workers, but he would do so only as leader of a disciplined and trusting set of people.

The disappointment at Serge Island was more of a lesson than a deterrent. Bustamante quite enjoyed winning over a crowd, but he seemed even happier matching wits with employers, using skilful argument and even bluff in order to win improvements for those whom he represented. He would fight to the end and be gracious in defeat, but he was deeply hurt if anyone mistrusted his sincerity. Yet no man was as quick to forgive even someone who had personally offended him.

The Serge Island incident must have had an influence on workers in other parts of Jamaica. Soon afterwards there were reports of work stoppages in various parishes. The whole island was restive. In Black River demands were made by the lightermen who refused to load cargo unless they were give two shillings per ton instead of one shilling and three pence. Waterfront workers in Savanna-la-mar followed suit. Workers everywhere were restive, but as wages were so low and jobs so scarce, a few pennies extra satisfied them – but only for a time. Though no work stoppage was long-drawn-out, each one was driving the situation nearer to the boiling point.

In Kingston that January, the street discussions by day and by night centred more on the need for jobs. Those who had employment found it hard to make ends meet. Those without work were in even greater difficulty and more than once before the month was out a crowd of unemployed men got together and marched to protest outside Headquarters House on Duke Street where the Legislative Council sat. On one occasion, the marchers were addressed by Hon. A.B. Lowe, the Legislative Council member for St. James. A black man, he was described by some as having Maroon ancestry. He had fairly large holdings at Sign where I had stayed earlier while in Montego Bay, and he was well-educated, able to speak on equal terms with people at all levels. He promised to make representations concerning the plight of the unemployed, and he did, both in and out of the Council.

While Lowe worked on the local scene, Bustamante decided to extend his representation to the British Parliament. On January 26 we sat down together and wrote a letter to Major Clement Attlee, Leader of the Labour Opposition in the House of Commons, later to be the Prime Minister who succeeded Sir Winston Churchill, because, as Mr B. wrote in part:

> . . . the Secretary of State's knowledge of conditions is too scanty for anyone to size up the situation . . . I merely write in the interest of my people . . . that the Secretary of State may have a broader knowledge of some of the conditions that now exist here and may seem fit to have a Commission sent out to investigate . . . We are surrounded with misery, poverty and sickness through low wages and unemployment and these ills have been increasing for a number of years and so one cannot blame the present Government entirely. Nevertheless, with the existing callous Government, matters have gone from bad to worse. . . The people are suffering from hunger, and if they dare to make peaceful manifestation, the police clubs are broken upon their heads and limbs. There have been strikes here and there: trouble is brewing, there is a volcanic feeling . . . the people are loyal to their King . . . but no one can tell when their patience will come to an end.

A week later we wrote another letter to George Griffiths of the Labour Party in which Bustamante described the conditions in Jamaica. We felt that Members of the British Parliament should be given a factual report from the people's point of view rather than be guided only by the Governor's official account. In calling for the visit of a Royal Commission to investigate, Bustamante pointed to a scene in which:

> Thousands upon thousands of able-bodied men willing to work, over-run the towns and districts, hungry and ragged from want of employment . . .Thousands of children . . . not being able to go to school from the lack of food and clothing; some are weak-legged and bow-legged from want of nourishment . . . I estimate 100,000 people starving and on the verge of starvation, the population is being wasted away from tuberculosis, chiefly from the lack of proper food caused through unemployment and sweated labour wages . . .unemployment is rampant. . .taxation destroying us . . . the situation is critical, it needs a specialist, but there is none in Jamaica . . . It is the duty of our Mother Government to send a Royal Commission to investigate and not just to treat the people of this country as if they were mere squatters in British territory.

The letter ended on a prophetic note: 'The pot of discontent is boiling . . . Today it has reached the brim, tomorrow it may overflow . . .'

Disappointed by the lack of response from the British parliamentarians, Bustamante turned to the British press. He wrote a letter dated March 19, 1938 to the *Manchester Guardian* and sent copies to Members of the House of Commons. The letter appeared in the *Guardian* on April 8 with the sub-head 'Call for a Commission of Enquiry'. It stirred up response in the British House of Commons and consternation in Jamaica. The letter repeated most of the points already made, but there were some additions, for example,

> . . . Things have been so bad that a short time ago, hundreds of ragged men, women and children marched to the doors of the prison in Kingston, pleading for admittance so that they might get food. These things seem to be hidden from the Secretary of State for the Colonies. If they are not, why does he not take some steps to see that these conditions are ameliorated?

and:

> I have used every effort through the press, the Governor, and public meetings to draw attention to the dreadful condition of the masses, but with no avail. I have been making it my duty to bring these conditions to the Mother Government through Labour Members in the House of Commons and the English press. In doing so, of course, I appreciate the

> fact that I became a marked man in Jamaica but what greater good can one attempt than to fight for the less fortunate, and I am not afraid.

Bustamante also repeated his call for a Commission of Enquiry. It has been suggested that this letter was, to some extent, responsible for the appointment of the Royal Commission, headed by Lord Moyne, later in the year.

On April 13 the *Daily Gleaner* carried a front page story from England. Datelined April 12 and sent by special cable, it read:

> In the House of Commons today, questions were raised as to the social conditions obtaining in Jamaica at the present time.
>
> It was stated that thousands of children of school age are roaming the island, unable to go to school owing to a lack of clothing and that men, women and children have been pleading for admission to prison in order to be fed, and escape other privations.
>
> The matter is being featured in some of the London newspapers and cables have been sent to Jamaica asking whether the statements are correct and for further details, if any.

Publication of this news item staggered officials in Jamaica. They expressed surprise at the development and said they knew nothing of the conditions described. The Governor sent a cable to England denying the existence of bad conditions and a published statement referred to 'a demonstration of school-children at Dinthill and they certainly all looked well-fed and well-dressed . . .'

On April 14 the *Daily Gleaner* published a report giving some of the attempts that had been made to ease the conditions of school children. The paper also published a copy of the following letter that we had sent to the Governor:

> Sir,
>
> It has always been my relentless policy to accept consequences and even pay the penalty, and so I would not like you to be wondering who is the person who has forwarded information to the Members of the House of Commons regarding the desperate social and economical conditions of the middle class and the masses of this island . . .
>
> I hasten to manifest to you that I am the person, chiefly because the Editor of a Kingston newspaper wrote . . . that it is some irresponsible person in the newspaper world of Kingston that has sent out these

reports, and he wonders if nothing can be done to prevent such criminally sensational reports to go out of the island. Your Excellency, what he really means is that the truth should not leave the island, so that poverty and all the accompanying ills should not be known in England. At the cost of martyrdom it must be known.

I fear nothing, I fear no one; my report can stand the acid test of investigation; I wrote from knowledge, not hearsay as some people do.

Alex Bustamante
1A Duke Street
Kingston

The debate was furious, but within a week the defenders of the status quo were stopped in their tracks. Without warning, labour troubles erupted where they might least have been expected – at the recently established Frome Central Sugar Factory in Westmoreland. Here there was work, for the giant English firm, Tate and Lyle, was busy consolidating the twenty-four estates it had acquired into one central operation, the West Indies Sugar Company (WISCO). Hearing of the enterprise, workers had flocked to the site in numbers far greater than the company needed. And there was double trouble because those who did manage to get jobs were being paid at rates below those given to road maintenance labour.

The Government's Public Works Department was paying a daily rate of three shillings and threepence while Frome was paying one shilling and three pence a day for men and sevenpence halfpenny a day for women. In addition, it was reported that the wage bills were paid too late on Saturdays for the workers to reach the food shops for their weekly purchases.

The 'commencement of sorrows' took place in April when workers at the new Tate and Lyle enterprise attacked the pay office, declaring that they would not do any more work unless they were paid at the rate of four shillings a day. At the first sign of trouble, the police were summoned and order was temporarily restored. But as April turned into May the attitude of the workers hardened. On May 3 they issued an ultimatum to the company: "Four shillings a day, or else today is going to be a day!" Again the police were summoned and in the general melee which ensued, four people were shot and killed, nine were seriously injured and eighty arrested. It was the worst episode in the catalogue of disturbances for that period.

That very night, as soon as he heard what was happening, Bustamante called me to accompany him to Frome. I in turn called a relative, Clement Blackwood, to join us and we travelled all night with Bustamante at the wheel, pressing on as fast as he could. The mission was urgent and I had responded to my boss's invitation to travel with him without hesitation. But as we covered the bumpy, winding roads I began to mull over the fact that we were going into a serious battle without being asked by anyone to intervene. Neither workers nor management were expecting us. We were simply reacting to a call of conscience, fired by one man's burning desire to go to the aid of his fellow men and women.

At dawn, almost at the end of our journey, Mr B stopped to perform an act of kindness which others might have ignored. In the dim light, we saw a policeman riding slowly on a horse. Walking next to the horse was a barefoot man whose handcuffed hands were tied with a piece of rope. The policeman held the other end.

As we passed the two men, Bustamante suddenly stopped the car, got out, walked up to them and asked what the man had done. The policeman replied, "Dem say him tief yam."

Busta shook a kindly finger at the accused and advised him, "Go along quietly and don't give the officer any trouble." Then turning to the policeman, he looked up at the drizzling rain and said, "You are going to get wet. Here is some money. Buy yourself some white rum to prevent a cold."

The constable thanked Bustamante and then said, "But after all, me never see him tief no yam!" and with that he untied the prisoner, took off the handcuffs and rode away.

Busta then said to the man, "Now, in future, if you want yam, see that you plant it yourself."

As we neared Frome, the tension thickened. We arrived in daylight, without much ceremony, and there, left on the ground, we found the dead bodies of three men and one pregnant woman with the unborn child protruding from her open stomach. We were appalled by this ugly scene and marvelled at the callousness of the authorities who could leave bodies lying for hours without even the preliminary steps for a decent burial. Bustamante himself consoled the woman's relatives and contributed to arrangements for her funeral.

Busta introduced himself to the workers and offered to lead them against the management. He hardly needed an introduction, for the workers had already heard of his reputation and while there was no consensus, there was an overall agreement that, at least for the time being, they would leave matters in his hands. The workers had refused the meagre increase which had been offered them They had also asked to be paid on Fridays instead of Saturdays but this also had met with a refusal.

While Bustamante tried to meet with the managers, I spent the time talking with the workers and having a look at this massive project that represented the biggest single investment made in Jamaica by any company up to 1938. So much had been said about this operation that it was no wonder that workers had flocked from miles away hoping to be employed. There was something of elegance about the buildings and facilities constructed for the managers but at first, and for some time afterwards, the accommodation provided for the workers matched the hovels that were called barracks on other sugar estates in Jamaica.

The first resident head of the new enterprise at Frome was an Englishman with a sparkling personality, quite aristocratic in manner and pleasingly friendly, unlike the condescending types usually sent to the colonies up to that time. His name was Robert Kirkwood and his wife was a niece of Sir Leonard Lyle (later Lord Lyle), president of Tate & Lyle. Kirkwood was later to play an important and influential role in Jamaica's business, politics and agriculture, in particular, by holding the top positions in the sugar industry. He later became Chairman of the

Sugar Manufacturers Association, holding that position for over a quarter of a century. He was subsequently knighted for his services. Kirkwood often crossed swords with Bustamante but on this occasion he was not the man with whom Busta was to negotiate.

The person appointed by Kirkwood to take charge of management was a former Director of Agriculture, A.C. Barnes, who showed a stubborn unwillingness to discuss the workers' demands. His position was that he had told the workers what they could or could not have and that there was no need to talk to anyone. The workers would have to return to their jobs or be starved into submission. Busta was incensed at this posture and virtually forced his way into Barnes's office, taking with him a delegation of the striking workers. He asked to be shown the records and management did acquiesce. Bustamante insisted that the demands were justified and then he addressed the workers who agreed to leave their destiny in his hands.

But the hard-liners in management could not be persuaded. With the government on their side and the police armed and ready to back them up, they had the upper hand over the disgruntled but disorganised workforce. Eventually we were obliged to inform the workers that a different strategy would have to be found. Rather than beating their heads against a brick wall or a series of batons, they would have to band themselves together and be armed with facts and figures rather than stones and machetes.

Most of the workers agreed to try the new tactics, and so the strike was partially settled. Some one hundred workers had been locked up in jail in Savanna-la-Mar, and Bustamante tried to bail them, but this was refused. We hurriedly returned to Kingston where he obtained the services of lawyer E.R.D.Evans who went down to defend them.

There were other workers so angry that they continued to cause disruptions and disturbances after we had left for Kingston. This brought on further police action which, together with threats to evict workers from their estate-owned accommodation, resulted in a grudging, gradual return to work.

The Frome situation, like the Serge Island strike, was strong proof of the need for solidarity among the workers. On the way home, we discussed the dilemma facing the workers all over the island and concluded that it would be far more effective to have a union with all workers acting as one, rather than fighting separate battles. Dividing the workers' movement into different categories and different trades was not the best way to fight. Others had been following that path, but it was clear that such a strategy could not work against an employer class welded together by a single purpose – to preserve the status quo. Out of this was born the idea of a blanket union for the workers of Jamaica.

News of what happened at Frome had reached the city before us and there was great excitement. Back in Kingston, Bustamante spoke to cheering thousands in Victoria Park, Kingston Race Course (now National Heroes Circle) and at street corners well-known as public meeting spots for St William Grant. He told the people of the troubles in Westmoreland, the plight of the workers, the cruelty of the employers and the unbridled force used by some policemen who had killed even a pregnant woman, leaving her ruptured body on the ground. He vowed that he would fight for the cause of the poor struggling masses of this country and warned that if something was not done by the authorities to help them, trouble would spread from Negril Point to Morant Point.

A few days later, at another meeting at Kingston Race Course, he told the crowd of a rumour that he was to be arrested. He said that if that were the case, they could send only one policewoman to arrest him and he would go quietly but when he came out he would make history for Jamaica. He knew he would suffer but he was determined, and his action would break the back of cowardice and oppression in this country. He warned that he would continue to agitate and agitate until Governor Denham went or until raggedness and starvation were almost eliminated in Jamaica.

He also told the crowds of the support for the strikers that had come from such agencies as the Jamaica Progressive League. The head of the Kingston branch of the JPL, W.G. McFarlane, had wired his

New York headquarters for assistance and money had been collected to secure legal help for those who had been arrested and to aid the families of the dead and the wounded.

McFarlane sought to engage the services of Norman Manley for defence of the workers at their trial, but that was not possible. Manley, like other leading barristers-at-law all over the world, had for years been retained by large firms and affluent individuals to handle their legal affairs on a permanent basis. 'Retainers' were renewable each year and should it occur that two opposing parties had both retained Manley in this way, then whichever one had paid the retainer on the earlier date, would be entitled to his services. It so happened that the West Indies Sugar Company was one of the firms that had retained Norman Manley and, therefore, when the dispute arose, he was obliged to sit in court at Savanna-la-Mar watching proceedings on the employer's behalf. Unfortunately for him, this did not help his reputation later as a supporter of the people since, for some circles, it appeared as though he was against the interests of the workers.

Lawyer E.R.D. Evans did defend the strikers, as Mr B. had arranged. However, in spite of his arguments, the workers were all found guilty and sent to prison for rioting.

While this was going on, Bustamante and St William Grant were holding meetings all over the place. Night and day, as Bustamante echoed the cry of the Frome workers for 'A Dollar a Day!' he painted graphic pictures of the brutality. In answer, the crowds would shout their disgust and pledge to fight not only their own cases but for that of any worker or workers coming under pressure from the government or the employers. He promised that he would devote his time, his energy, his money and his life to fighting their cause as long as they would act in unison and abide by his advice. He said that this would be his constant message to those in the cane fields as well as the waterfront, where stevedores were required to lift heavy loads at the rate of ninepence an hour for 'ship men' and eightpence an hour for 'dock men'.The workers' response was tremendous. Apart from the huge crowds attending the public meetings, we had groups and individuals coming every day to see Bustamante at the Duke Street office. Ice vendors, curio sellers, street cleaners, casual workers and the unemployed were among hundreds seeking his assistance. He would give them all a patient hearing while I recorded the facts and helped to reassure them that action would be taken to ease their burdens.

Never had any of the island's public meetings been so wildly enthusiastic or so threatening to the powers that be. Never were so many workers so unified and never, since the heyday of Marcus Garvey, had there been such a clear expression of faith in a single man. This is probably why the critics began to call Bustamante the 'Dollar a Day Dictator'. Years later, the *Daily Gleaner,* in reviewing the events of 1938, commented that Bustamante had inflamed the crowds with violent speeches. But it was not violence that Bustamante was preaching. Rather it was the replacement of disorganised resentment with organised resistance.

6

May Twenty-third to Twenty-ninth

TUESDAY, MAY 24 WAS EMPIRE DAY, a holiday when schoolchildren holding little Union Jacks would assemble, listen to a lecture about the glory of the British Empire, and sing Rule Britannia and other patriotic songs of the Mother Country before being served buns and lemonade. Then school would be over for the day and they would go home, waving their flags.

Most people expected that the Monday before the holiday would be a regular working day. But from the beginning, there were those who had seen clearly the signs that 'any day now' there might be a stunning upheaval in the city of Kingston. Among those who saw and recognised the danger, was a young woman who trembled inwardly at the thought — that was me. And there was a tall man shaking his head in a passionate demand for justice — that was Bustamante.

Many people think that the events of that memorable week in May all started on that Monday. But that was not the case. The first trouble on the Kingston waterfront came two weeks before, on Monday the 9th when workers refused to load the M/V Costa Rica because it had come from Curaçao with its own workers to unload the two hundred tons of cargo to be delivered. At the same time, the dockers took the opportunity to protest for another reason: they were not being paid for their lunch-time. Bustamante went to the wharf concerned and spoke with the management on the workers' behalf. Although there was no formal union, he persuaded management to pay for the lunch-time.

During that same week, newspaper reports of the Legislative Council meetings disclosed that the Public Works Department would soon be starting new projects that would offer jobs outside Kingston. Despite this, people continued to stream into the city from the countryside, looking for work, especially as it had also been announced that additional funds would be spent on the Trench Pen (now Trench Town) project which had been started the year before.

The Friday of that week was the 13th of the month. Then, as now, many held to the superstition that a Friday falling on the 13th meant trouble. On this particular Friday about three hundred jobless men, with nobody leading them, began to march a second time to Headquarters House, to complain that they could not find work at Trench Pen. An official of the Colonial Secretariat apologised for the disappointment and told the men to go to May Pen Cemetery along the Spanish Town Road, and to return to him if they did not get some work at that site. So they marched to the cemetery, but when they got there the place was literally a ghost town – no PWD personnel, no government official, no work.

The disappointed men marched back to the city, accompanied by a large contingent of police. The thirsty marchers made a brief stop along the way to refresh themselves with sugar cane from a passing truck but there was no disorder. Later in the day, Bustamante spoke to a discontented crowd at North Parade. He denounced the Governor and the Corporation contractors and said that the Elected Members had done nothing for the island. However, he left the meeting on hearing that there was new unrest at the waterfront and went to hear the grievances of the workers.

There was more trouble at Trench Pen two days later. The contractors intended to employ about sixty men that morning but hundreds arrived for the jobs. They began to be disorderly and threatened the contractor. Bustamante climbed a tree to speak to them and brought disorder to an immediate end when he shouted, "Peace, men! Peace be still." As if by magic the crowd turned to hear him. He promised to have a conference with the Mayor in an effort to find additional work but he was summoned instead to the waterfront where the wharf workers were poised to make their demands for an eight-hour day. Bustamante advised them to remain orderly and promised the crowd that he would take up the matter with the companies involved. Then he departed for another meeting at North Parade, sponsored by the Social Reconstruction League, at which he was due to speak. There he was given a rousing welcome and spoke at length to the crowd on the need to have unity if the movement was to be successful.

On Monday, May 16, we had hardly started work at the office when we heard that things were getting out of hand again at Trench Pen. By the time we got there, the Mayor and Deputy Mayor were on the spot and Busta joined them in appealing to those who were not yet working to hold on a little longer for their turn to come. The Town Clerk promised that some two hundred and fifty more jobs would be available, but it was only Bustamante's plea for patience that averted a violent demonstration.

By Thursday, the halting confusion of the previous days at the waterfront seemed to be taking a specific direction. About two hundred dock workers employed by the United Fruit Company had gone on strike, refusing to load any cargo until their demands for wage increases were met. A deputation from the waterfront had waited on Bustamante at the Duke Street office and had asked for his assistance in their struggle. By this time he had already made up his mind. He told them that whether they had asked him or not, it was his intention to join in the struggle because it was for a just cause. Then, turning to me, he asked if I would go with him. Immediately I replied that whatever happened I was prepared to stick with him and the workers. It was not a difficult decision for me. By then, I had developed a tremendous loyalty to Bustamante and I was convinced that he was on the right track.

Within minutes I had cleared my desk and was off to the United Fruit Company's wharf with Bustamante and the group of determined workers. The company was the largest buyer of bananas in those times and a large proportion of each week's shipment went from their wharf in Kingston by a method I had not seen in Montego Bay. Here in Kingston, the railway lines ran right down to the wharf to shipside. And here I was seeing train-loads of bananas being turned back and the ships leaving empty to go to Port Antonio for loading.

On Friday morning, May 20, Bustamante spoke with the managers who said they would not consider any increase until work was resumed. Busta relayed the information to the workers and advised them to remain off the job, saying he was a hundred per cent for labour and that he would lead the fight against employers. No firm decision was made then, but on Saturday the dock workers went on strike. Ships came in, but none went out. All weekend Busta busied himself with meeting after meeting. I thought at times that he might be near exhaustion, but he just kept going, even stronger. Then on the Sunday there was a meeting on the waterfront. Some of the workers were wavering.

Busta warmed up to the issue and told the men that they had to make up their minds once and for all what they were going to do. They should stand together and not break ranks because their cause was just and "because your children want shoes, just as theirs. Your women want shoes, as theirs; and even the policemen who cannot speak for themselves, want better wages." The crowd agreed and Busta declared, "Now you have made your decision. I respect your decision, now let me respect your behaviour. This is a war and you cannot expect to win a war if the soldiers are divided one against the other."

And so to Monday, May 23. On my way to work I noticed a lot of rubbish on the streets – rubbish that was usually cleared before dawn by the Kingston and St Andrew Corporation street-cleaners. Some business places were closed but because it was still early in the day the full impact of the situation did not reach my mind. I went on to the office and, after a while, I realised that it was past the time that Mr B. usually arrived. Then someone came in to say that 'hell a pop' at the waterfront. I knew right away that Busta must be in the thick of it, so I closed the office and along with a friend of mine, Thelma Deslandes, headed out knowing well that we would quickly find out exactly where the centre of the action was.

Thelma and I soon reached the Standard Fruit Company's wharf where I heard Busta and St William Grant telling the demonstrators to march up to Victoria Park where there would be more space for the thousands who would be gathered to impress the government.

I worked my way up to him and said that I was going to march with the crowd. He managed a smile as he said, "Stand by me, but be careful." The crowd moved off with Busta and St William Grant at the head, and Thelma and I close behind them.

As the huge crowd assembled at the Parade, Bustamante mounted Queen Victoria's statue and began to address the people. He told them that their show of strength was all that he needed to go forward and do all he could for them. At the end of his speech he called upon the people to go home in peace, to be sure to maintain their unity and to depend upon him to do the best he could. As he descended from the statue, a squad of policemen, headed by Inspector Orrett, marched on the crowd. Orrett pulled his revolver and gave the command to the police, "Click your heels and aim!" Then he ordered the people to disperse. Baring his chest Bustamante confronted Orrett and declared, "If you are going to shoot, shoot me, but leave these defenceless, hungry people alone."

The inspector was speechless. The policemen lowered their arms and I stood there almost frozen to the spot, wondering if the end had come even as Mr Bustamante was beginning the work he had planned. I wanted to move away, but the crowd stood firm with the discipline that Bustamante had so often preached. Before Orrett could say another word, Busta called upon the people to sing the National Anthem and as God Save the King rang out from the mass of discordant voices, the police were forced to stand at attention and could advance no further. Bustamante then moved away with the large crowd following him.

At that moment I realized that something new was happening in Jamaica; that the poor had passed the stage when they could be bullied and pressed into submission by guns and bayonets. This feeling of defiance was contagious and I somehow became infused with the courage to stand with the fighters. For me the hour of decision had arrived and there could be no turning back.

After the meeting at Queen Victoria's statue, there was rioting in the streets of the city and there were running battles between the forces of law and order and the surging mass. Bottles, stones, bricks, rained from the crowd and were answered with bayonets, batons and rifles. The casualties were many. A mother looking out of her upstairs window was shot and her children injured as the police assumed mistakenly that stones had fallen from that direction. People crouched behind zinc gates and hurled crumbling bricks and pieces of mortar at uniformed men alighting from army wagons with fixed bayonets. Shortly after midnight, the shots had ceased to ring out and all was quiet.

The occurrences immediately after the meeting at the statue are not the only ones worthy of mention. In 1977, the Jamaica Information Service (for some reason I have never been able to explain, it was then known as the Agency for Public Information) put together a publication giving overall coverage of the day's events which is helpful in getting a picture. The following shortened extracts describe the turbulence which took place in other parts of the city:

> From an early hour, mobs began to collect and parade the streets of Kingston. Dustbins were overturned and their contents scattered on the streets, shops and bakeries were attacked and goods and money stolen.
>
> At 6 a.m. every available member of the Police Force was paraded at the Central Police Station under the Inspector General in charge of Kingston who thus had at his disposal a force of about 250 officers and men armed with batons and rifles. The transport unit was strengthened by the addition of a number of lorries capable of carrying twenty-five men each.
>
> Between the hours of 6 and 8 a.m., the Police were able to control the situation by dispatching parties of ten to twenty men to different

points. However, as time passed, the mobs were much increased. They began to threaten shopkeepers with violence unless they closed their shops and released their assistants; and as a result, all shops in the centre of the city had to close.

Persons of all classes going to business were set upon, public property was destroyed, streets blocked and tramcars attacked. A hostile mob entered the sewage pumping station and drove out the staff, and another took possession of the Gold Street Power Station of the Jamaica Public Service Company.

Shortly before 9.30 a.m. the Inspector General of Police requested military aid. Two platoons of the First Battalion of the Sherwood Foresters proceeded to the city at 10.30 a.m., and four additional platoons followed them shortly afterwards. They drove out the mob from the Gold Street power house and armed guards were posted at the railway station, the headquarters of the telephone company, the Public Buildings, the Sewage Pumping Station and the Electrical Service stations.

At about 10.30 a.m. the police received a report of a large mob advancing from Smith Village (now known as Denham Town) towards the railway station. With a force of forty-five men, the Inspector in charge of Kingston proceeded to the spot and was confronted by a hostile and turbulent crowd estimated to be some 3,500 strong. He extended his party across the street and gave the order to load. At the same time he perceived another crowd, rather more numerous, bearing down upon him from the opposite direction. At the rear of this crowd was a sub-inspector with a party of fifteen men in a lorry who succeeded in forcing his way through the crowd and joining forces with his superior officer. In the very nick of time a detachment of the Sherwood Foresters arrived upon the scene followed shortly afterwards by two lorry loads of police and the combined forces succeeded in dispersing both crowds without the use of firearms.

At about the same time in another quarter of the city, a mob of two hundred attempted to storm the Public Service Electric Light and Tram Depot in Orange Street.They were kept from entering the premises by the staff who closed the big iron gates. An Inspector and twenty men succeeded in dispersing the crowd by means of a baton charge.

By 11.00 a.m., all transport services had ceased to operate, practically all labour had been suspended and business was at a complete standstill . . .

From noon until nightfall, a series of military truck patrols of the Sherwood Foresters were sent out from the Central Police Station

> through the principal thoroughfares and were largely instrumental in restoring order.
>
> During the day. all units of the Local Forces were mobilised and a call was made for Special Constables, In Kingston, two hundred were enrolled. They shared with the police and Local Forces the task of patrolling and guarding the city. In St Andrew a further two hundred split up into parties and, in their own cars, patrolled the residential areas during the night.

Other exciting events of that historic day are recorded in different books and in documents in the archives; and no one with a sense of history and its importance to Jamaicans today should go through life without at least one look at some of them. I think it a pity that so many so often take for granted the precious legacy of 1938. I was at centre stage when that history was being made and yet, throughout my years in the labour movement, I always found it inspiring and energising to look back upon the bravery of the workers and the sacrifices which those downtrodden people were prepared to make in order to rise up and win the respect and freedom that had so long been denied them and which we all enjoy today.

I cannot now recall all the events I was involved in during the evening of that turbulent day. I cannot even remember whether I went back to the office with Thelma or headed straight home after the Victoria Park meeting. It was probably the latter, and I certainly would have gone away quietly, turning down any offer that Bustamante would have made to ensure my safety by riding in his car. Had he tried to do that, there can be no doubt that we would have been surrounded by his followers and yet another crowd situation would have developed.

The next morning, Tuesday, May 24, Empire Day and a holiday, I was at home when I learnt that the whole city was again on the march. Bustamante had been trying to hold meetings at different points in the city, but at each attempt the police would break up the gathering which they deemed to be an unlawful assembly. Then a friend came to tell me that Bustamante and St William Grant had gone to the Fire Brigade Station on Sutton Street, just facing the back entrance to the Central Police Station. I knew there might be trouble, because the firemen had been talking about strike action, and Busta had been trying to dissuade them from that course.

I had to be there, for I had made up my mind that, through thick and thin, I would be at Bustamante's side, and particularly in a crisis. Hurriedly I got dressed and took a bus to the western fringe of town, then walked the rest of the way to the corner of Hanover and Sutton Streets. By the time I got there, Busta had already told the disgruntled workers and a crowd of onlookers that he would speak with the Mayor of Kingston about the situation and that strike action should be withheld as it would be disastrous in case of a fire in the city. Just as I was moving to get closer, Inspector Orrett and four policemen appeared and arrested Bustamante and St William Grant. Orrett said, "We've got you where we want you now. Come!" and they took both men in custody.

Neither of the two men offered any resistance to the police, but St. William, who was never able to remain silent even in the face of great odds, protested loudly and was subjected to a terrible beating with batons. There was no need for such brutal conduct which was in complete contrast to their cautious approach to Bustamante who told them, "Don't any of you dare to touch me with your batons." It must also have occurred to the policemen that the same crowd that stood and watched Grant maltreated would have exploded in anger had they laid hands on the man whom they regarded as their leader and representative. To this day, I cannot forget that even while feeling anxiety and resentment at Bustamante's arrest, I could not hold back the tears at the sight of the cruelty meted out to St William Grant — and for no sensible reason at all.

I followed Bustamante and Grant to the Central Police Station, just a few chains away from the scene of the arrest. Busta was calm and self-possessed. As the policemen milled, about he took a gun from his waist and, giving it to a Corporal Thompson, remarked, "Your Inspector did not have enough sense to disarm me. I could have used it on him." There was a sudden silence, then he smiled as he reached into his pocket and, offering to stand bail for himself and Grant, produced a large wad of paper money, which I learned later was about five hundred pounds. At this, an English soldier standing nearby, blurted out, "Dammit, that bloke has a whole bank on him!"

The station erupted into laughter at this, but I could see no humour in it, for I was outraged that Bustamante had been arrested while on a mission of peace. I knew it was an attempt by the Government to intimidate him, in the hope that by treating the leader in that way they would get the workers to lose heart and desert their own cause, but I was confident that Bustamante and the people would triumph in the end.

When the police refused to give Busta his own bail, a number of friends and supporters stepped forward to bail the two, but this also was refused. Both men were detained in the lock-up, facing charges of sedition, inciting unlawful assembling and obstructing Inspector Orrett in the lawful execution of his duty. As Busta afterwards told it, even the board that prisoners had to lie on was taken out of his cell to make it more uncomfortable for him. Furthermore, he was stripped down to his underwear in the effort to humiliate him and to break his spirit. It didn't work. He sent a message to me to get his lawyer, Allan Wynter, and then refused to speak to any of the policemen who were asking questions. For two days, he would not eat any of the food they offered him and when one policeman threatened to force-feed him, he loudly defied them.

When the news of the arrest of Bustamante and St William Grant began to spread,the upheavals broke out again and casualties mounted. By the afternoon more workers had joined the demonstrations and business activity in the city came to a stop. Outside Kingston, woodcutters in Glengoffe laid down their axes and went on strike as did workers in Bushy Park. In Montego Bay, banana loading came to a standstill. The Governor had hastily summoned the Legislative Council in order to seek, and obtain, its sanction to declare a State of Emergency.

As time passed, it was feared that workers would storm the Central Police Station and attempt to release the two prisoners so, at 3 a.m. on the Thursday, they were moved to the General Penitentiary. Bustamante was given a room in which an Englishman who had committed himself had served his sentence some time before. At that point, Mr B. was told that he could have meals sent in to him but he told them, "I am in prison and I am going to eat prison food!"

In the midst of all this I had contacted not only lawyer Wynter but also Mr Ross Livingston, another of Bustamante's personal attorneys. I also went to barrister J.A.G. Smith, who informed me that whether I had come or not he had intended to visit Mr Bustamante and to offer his services. All three had applied for bail and all three had been refused. Norman Manley had not been in Kingston when the troubles started that week because he was at the trial of the Frome workers, attending court on behalf of the West Indies Sugar Company, but when he got the news he immediately rushed to the city to see what he could do.

The story of how Manley became involved was told by Sir Herbert MacDonald in an interesting radio broadcast during the 1980s. This is his account of what happened:

> I used to work at Fred L. Myers & Son, at the foot of Harbour Street, and the mob closed us down, so I decided to go home. I just couldn't go home the way I wanted to; I had to go the way the mob decided I should go, because they had taken charge of King Street; they'd taken charge of Harbour Street and all the rest of it.
>
> Well, I drove home, but on the way I stopped at Wolmer's Girls' School and told the headmistress of all the trouble that was going on and suggested that she should close down the school. She didn't agree with me there and then, but eventually did. I took a neighbour's girl home and next door to me lived Mr Leslie Clerk, the famous piano tuner. At the gate was Leslie with Mrs Edna Manley.
>
> I stopped and asked them if they had heard what was happening downtown. Mrs Manley told me, "No," then she said,"Well, would you like to drive me down and let me see what's happening?" I wasn't too keen on doing it, but I decided, and I drove her down – went to the Royal Mail Wharf, as near as we could get. She then decided that she wanted to send a telegram to her husband, N.W. Manley, who was in Frome involved in the trouble down there. I said, "All right." We would

> drive up King Street and go to the Post Office. But we couldn't get near to King Street Post Office.
>
> So I said, "Let's go up to Cross Roads to send the telegram." She then said, "I think perhaps N.W. Manley is the only man who could restore some sort of order to what's going on down here." So we went to Cross Roads and then I discovered that neither she nor I had any money – both of us had given away every penny we had, and I asked the postmistress, Miss King, if she would trust me one-and-sixpence for the telegram, and she said, Yes. Mrs Manley sent the telegram to tell her husband that she thought he ought to come to Kingston. He replied later, telling her that he didn't understand the telegram – because of course down there they hadn't heard what was going on – but eventually he came up the same evening. The rest of it is, of course, history.

Mrs Manley was quite right in declaring that the immediate need was for order to be restored; and it is also true that her urgent call to Mr Manley made a difference to the situation that week. I did not know much about this happening at the time, for I was kept extremely busy, running the office single-handed and keeping communication going between Bustamante and his lawyers. My priority was securing legal help for Bustamante and Grant. I had seen what had happened to St William in front of a crowd on the street and I was wondering what might be Bustamante's fate behind bars and away from public notice.

Thirty years later, Manley himself recalled certain of the events of that time in history. He was replying to toasts on the occasion of his seventy-fifth birthday and said.

> I will never forget the day in May 1938 when I walked the ghost town of Kingston – May the 24th – and decided to take up the case of the Fire Brigade which was threatening to strike, with a deadline of 2 p.m. I will never forget how that night I sat with my wife under a great old tree, while we talked about what was happening – what was likely to be the fate of the people – and finally decided to offer my services to all the strikers in Jamaica, and to work to snatch good out of what looked like so grim a tangle of despair.

Edna Manley herself was involved in the waterfront strike. She and Aggie Bernard, a washerwoman who took in clothes for workers on visiting ships, helped to look after the relief meals for the workers on strike and other women volunteered to help as well. In answer to their appeals, contributions poured in for the dock labourers and arrangements were made to supply cooked meals for 1,500 persons daily and uncooked food as well. N.N. Nethersole, who later became a Minister of Finance and chief spirit behind the formation of the Bank of Jamaica, was one of the coordinators of the programme to collect food and money for the strikers.

With Bustamante in jail, Norman Manley became very active that same day, offering to help as mediator between the striking workers and the shipping companies. By this time, the whole waterfront was tied up. Manley had several meetings with interested parties and then went to the waterfront to address the workers, promising to negotiate with the shipping companies on their behalf. He told them that he would make a report on his progress the next day and asked that only the waterfront workers involved in the strike should attend.

Telling of what had transpired in his earlier talk with the shippers, Manley explained, "You have not chosen me as your leader, but there was a situation in which somebody had to come forward and say a word. I was told yesterday, not by one person, but by many people that you were not disposed to go back to work until your leader is released on bail. Mr Bustamante's case is in the hands of a great lawyer and great worker for the people, the Hon. J.A.G. Smith who is representing him today."

Mr. Manley also issued a statement which was published in the Gleaner the next day, Wednesday. It read:,

> I approached His Excellency the Governor today and received his assurance that Government were entirely serious in their desire that the people should have an opportunity of making representations and that their grievances should receive, by whatever body was concerned, the fullest consideration. If necessary, Government would be prepared to appoint a Conciliation Board where representatives of both sides could be heard and an attempt made to adjust matters; and I am convinced that . . . one of the greatest difficulties in the way of any desire on the part of Government to assist in these troubles is the difficulty of finding organised bodies that are willing to assist the labouring classes in

> putting forward their grievances . . .
>
> I pledge myself to serve their interests fairly and properly, and to give every assistance to see that reasonable and fair demands are met in a proper spirit. I can give this assurance that if any group will accept these services, or if they can find the services of any responsible person who is willing to assist them in putting forward their case, I am confident that they will be heard and that something will be done.

The next day, after more meetings with different parties, Manley returned to the waterfront to report what he had managed to do, but it was not enough. When he put forward the proposals of the shipping companies, an increase of threepence an hour which would bring shipmen up to eleven pence and dockmen up to tenpence an hour, the response was shouts of "We don't want it!"

Manley told them that he had done his best. He explained that increases in wages would inevitably be accompanied by increases in the cost of freight and, in turn, in the price of food, but the workers did not want to listen. They wanted their leader.

As the workers kept saying that they would not accept the wage increase, Manley told them, "I advise you to accept. This is a practical world, and when you have made a bargain and have got a fair raise and know that you have gone as far as you can get, it is better to get half a loaf than to die trying to get a full loaf, which you will never get."

The workers shouted,"We would rather die."

And Mr. Manley asked them, "What the hell will you die for?"

Then one of the workers, W.A. Williams, spoke up. "We cannot leave our welfare in the hands of other people. We cannot behold injustice triumph over justice. We have suffered this slavery system for many generations and now the time has come to shake ourselves from captivity. We don't want ten pounds an hour. We want Bustamante!"

Much as the workers needed a raise of pay, their overriding concern at that time was the release of Bustamante. They might have shown more consideration for Mr Manley's efforts, but at that time they were adamant that there would be no work until Bustamante was released. This response of the workers must have surprised many who thought that the men would forget Bustamante once they got what they wanted. As Manley himself wrote several years later in his memoirs, "The shippers had agreed to all my demands on the part of the workers. They were certain that this eliminated the demand for Bustamante's release and they were certain that once they got what they wanted, loyalty would seem less important . . . "

After the meeting with Manley, truckloads of workers drove through the city shouting to cheering onlookers,"No work! No work! We don't want shilling an hour. We want Bustamante!" And everywhere they scattered pamphlets which read:

> The Government of Jamaica in its efficiency has seen it fit to remove our leader Bustamante from our midst. This latest move is calculated to break our spirit as now we are without a leader, and the Government thinks we will readily give in and go back to slave labour with our tails between our legs. They are wrong in this thought, for we intend, and will show them that the soul of Bustamante is with us and we will not let this great effort fall to the ground by going back to earn starvation wages.
>
> We remember his words, "This is not a military revolution, this is a mental revolution." We will not forget those words; we are acting on them, so we will be orderly and peaceful until all employers decide to give us what is due. No longer do we mean to be fooled. The Government will not laugh at us.

Meanwhile, serious efforts were being made to secure the release of Busta and Grant from the General Penitentiary. J.A.G. Smith's application for their release was again refused in the Supreme Court and he proceeded to file a writ of Habeas Corpus. Norman Manley, after his failure to get the workers to accept the shippers' offer of threepence an hour, had gone to the General Penitentiary and assured Bustamante that no law was keeping him there. He also tried to persuade the Governor, Sir Edward Denham, and members of the Conciliation Board, that there would be no peace among the striking workers or in the country at large, until the Bustamante was released. He was right, because the unrest was spreading in the rural areas. In Highgate at the Charlottenburgh Estate, labourers abandoned their jobs when other strikers entered and forced them to join the movement. At Caymanas

Estate, too, the police had to be called in as workers threw up a blockade at the entrance.

On Saturday, May 28, Bustamante and Grant appeared for their third hearing, before the Supreme Court. J.A.G. Smith, acting on behalf of the accused, presented powerful arguments in support of the application for bail. He assured the Court that if Bustamante were released no further riots would occur. The Court agreed to release Bustamante on condition that Smith's assurances were further guaranteed by a number of affidavits including those of Mr Ross Livingston, Mr Norman Manley and Miss Beryl Murray who was at that time employed to lawyer Alan Wynter. This was done and Bustamante and St William Grant were free men.

On the very same day, Sir Edward Denham was taken ill and was later moved to Kingston Public Hospital. He was supposed to have gone on vacation leave some time before, but because of the unsettled situation he had been compelled to remain. The stress had been too much for him.

Immediately upon their release, Bustamante and Grant attended the Conciliation Board, which had been set up two days before to deal with the situation, to be apprised of what Manley had managed to work out on behalf of the workers. Busta went through it carefully and agreed to get the approval of the workers for the original increase plus overtime at double rates. The party then went on to the waterfront where the workers had been waiting patiently for some two hours. When they saw Bustamante, they went wild with joy. After a while, he raised his hands and called for total silence. "I want to hear a pin drop," he said.

Bustamante's speech that afternoon began, "Fellow-workers, the first thing I want you to do next week is to send to me at my office a deputation of three or four, including my friend, Mr W.A. Williams. I want to consult with Mr Williams and two or three others from among you. I want to shoot right away with the Union."

The applause that greeted this statement was deafening. We had all been saying that a strong and proper trade union was a necessary tool in the struggle. Mr Manley, too, had done some groundwork and had advised the workers that they should form a union as soon as possible.

However, at that time they had declared that Bustamante was the obvious leader and that nothing would be done unless and until he was released from jail. Now the time was ripe. Busta was free and the workers were ready to follow his leadership.

The Chief then expressed his gratitude to all those who had worked for his release and he had a special word about his cousin, Norman Manley. "I was glad that Mr Manley came down to enter the breach . . . Mr Manley came at a time when I did not ask him to come, but when I really needed his services. He volunteered to help getting me out of the Penitentiary and I appreciate it sincerely. If he had waited until I asked him, I would not have appreciated it so much; and when he told me that Mrs Manley, his wife, was doing something to help you, I was overwhelmed."

After that, Bustamante announced the wage increases that he had approved earlier in the day. This touched off wild scenes of dancing and lusty singing of the song, 'We will follow Bustamante till we die'. That was a phrase that was to fall from the lips of tens of thousands in the years to come. It would be sung throughout Jamaica and be regarded as the slogan and the spirit of the movement. As for me, it was a rare pleasure to see victory after such an exacting struggle. I was particularly happy with the loyalty of the workers who had steadfastly refused to sell out their leadership for a raise in their pay.

The next day, May 29, there was peace and quiet in the city. Work on the waterfront returned to normal and, for the first time in seven days, ships received their cargo at the Royal Mail Wharf, the Lascelles Wharf and the Number Two Pier.

7

Building a Union

THE VICTORY OF THE DOCK WORKERS was not the end of the struggle. The trials and triumphs of May 1938 were together the opening salvo of a long and complex battle to form trade unions and political parties; to choose appropriate social and economic objectives and to decide which path to follow at each crossroads along the way. However, the Colonial Government seemed to see the situation differently. In their view, they had only to silence Bustamante and all would be well.

When the magistrates agreed to release Bustamante and St Willliam Grant it was on the clear understanding that they would keep the peace and be of good behaviour. In the words of Paragraph 9 of the document which had to be signed by each of Busta's legal defenders, 'I am satisfied and it is my opinion that if Bustamante is released on bail no disorder will arise . . . '

This demand for good behaviour was amusing to me because, to my certain knowledge, Bustamante had always been of good behaviour. It was not he who stirred up trouble on the waterfront; it was already there. Only after the difficulties had erupted was he brought directly into the picture to articulate the grievances and to try for a settlement of the dispute. He had not been violent and had urged no one to engage in violent conduct or any other form of illegal behaviour. In fact, it was he who called for calm whenever there was an angry demonstration; and it was he who persuaded the firemen not to strike, but to negotiate.

Bustamante was never a negative or disruptive force. He was the leader of the oppressed and therefore the central figure whenever they cried out against oppressive conditions. He expressed their frustration, sounded aloud his warnings to the Government and called for sanity, equity, justice and peace. According to the authorities, Busta's behaviour was disruptive, seditious, unlawful and inciting. However, the workers had a different view; they believed in him, trusted him and wanted him to be their official leader.

I remember how they came in thousands on June 3, 1938, to gather below his offices on the corner of Duke Street and Water Lane and clamour for him to form a union to act on their behalf. But it was not easy for him to make the decision. He came out of his small private office and strode across to the balcony where he was greeted with cheers and he waved to the mob. Then turning back into the room, he called out to me, "Miss Longbridge, Miss Longbridge, they want me to form a union." Then he returned to the window and acknowledged the thunderous cheers, only to come back again to say, "Miss Longbridge, what shall I do?" He paced to and fro for a while,looking quite agitated and finally said, "Miss Longbridge, they want me to form a union, but if I do it the hand of every big man in this country is going to be raised against me." For a few moments, he paused in thought, then turned and strode back onto the balcony, this time to announce that he would organise the union. His hesitation can well be understood because there were many factors to consider, both personal and in the wider picture. But his sudden dramatic decision proved that he saw that the needs of the workers outweighed those considerations. He could not resist their cries for him to be their leader.

That indeed was the beginning of the BITU In the weeks after his release, Bustamante kept the peace all right. He and I spent many hours with lawyers and workers' representatives, steadily hammering out the foundation upon which the new organisation was to be built. There were many angles and details to consider. However, the Chief made clear to everyone looking to his leadership: "It is going to be a union the discipline of which will be almost that of the army, for without discipline we cannot succeed, and with disorder we will fail . . . It is impossible for me to promise you everything that you want now, and if I were to tell you that I would be deceiving you and leading you into the Red Sea." We all understood that principle and unanimously agreed to it.

While this organisational work was going on and without any prompting from us, discontent kept boiling up as furiously as before but this time it was more in the country parts than in the city. Only once during that time did we go to a troubled spot – Mandeville; and as usual, it was to restore calm and to urge the workers to have their cases dealt with in an orderly manner.

In the week after Bustamante's release, crowds of unemployed and striking workers all over the country massed together and roamed the streets, dislocating traffic, forcing those working to quit their posts, blocking roads, throwing up barricades and seeking support from anyone they met. During that week, local government employees in St James withdrew their labour. In St Catherine, labourers at Salt Pond went on the march. In St Elizabeth, noisy crowds congregated in Black River Square and schools at Santa Cruz were forced to close down. Workers in St Mary, at Fontabelle, Trinity, Brimmer Hall and Annotto Bay were demonstrating while in Portland the Member of the Legislative Council, H.E. Allan, was doing his best to soothe the discontented.

In the midst of the turmoil, Governor Denham died. He had undergone surgery at the Kingston Public Hospital on May 31 but two days later he passed away. The battleship, HMS *Ajax*, which had come to the island to help quell the disturbances, took his body out to sea and there his body was consigned to the deep. We were to find that his successor was a very different kind of man.

On the day before Denham's death, the Government announced a 25 per cent wage increase for its workers, warning at the same time that taxes would have to be increased to meet the cost. Then workers at Islington in St Mary became engaged in a major clash with the police.

The trouble erupted when farm labourers began a protest against their low wages. They complained that men were being paid two shillings and sixpence to fork a square of land and that women were getting one shilling for a day's work, which lasted from 7 a.m. to 5 p.m.

The disgruntled workers had appealed to our office for help but when Bustamante's intervention brought no immediate result, they took to the streets, smashing buildings and shops. The arrival of the police only made matters worse, and when they beat one of the protesters for refusing to give up a stick he was carrying, the situation further deteriorated. Thaddeus Smith, throwing stones from a trench, was shot through the heart. Caleb Barrett received a bullet in the eye and died on the spot. Archibald Franklin was bayoneted and Felix McLeggon wounded in the leg. They were taken away by the police and never lived to say what happened next.

The people of Islington have never forgotten that day and even now there is a monument that they raised to commemorate the sacrifices of those slain workers and others who demonstrated for better working conditions. The memorial tablet was unveiled by me in September 1963 at a ceremony chaired by the late MP, Wycliffe Martin.

Before the end of June, we had completed plans and launched a five union organisation under one umbrella. A Maritime Union included dock workers, banana carriers, longshoremen and others on the waterfront; a Transport Workers Union was for tram and railway workers, mechanics and chauffeurs; a Factory Workers Union covered workers in industry; the Municipal Workers Union was for Government workers' interests and the General Workers Union was for all agricultural workers not falling into the other categories.

When it came to the point of naming the parent union, there was only a brief discussion. Most of the organising members declared that the union had to be clearly distinguishable from those already in existence and should be so designated that the workers would know for sure that it was into Bustamante's hands and none other that they were placing their trust and their fate. There was also the possibility of union leaders jostling for position at the expense of the workers' solidarity. The solution to these possible problems, it was felt, was to name the union in honour of Bustamante and to make him President for Life in order to discourage rivalry among aspiring leaders. When these considerations were put before the workers themselves, the support was unanimous and enthusiastic.

This decision was the result of the realities of the time, the state of affairs existing in Jamaica and the absolute faith, hope, trust and confidence that the workers had in Bustamante. Today, many would challenge the correctness of a person being named to hold office for his lifetime. But, as it turned out, the workers' judgment was correct. Until the day of the Chief's death, the great majority of the Union members and officers would have had no other person at the head of the organisation. My own unwavering support of the Chief and my intimate contact with the workers led to my having a share of the support of the workers. I was made Treasurer of the Union and, although not elected for life, I have managed to hold the post from 1938 until now – 1997.

The Bustamante Industrial and Tradesmen's Union started life at 30 Duke Street and Bustamante was obliged to finance organising expenses, such as travelling and stationery, from his own pocket. However, growth was so rapid that we soon moved to more spacious accommodation at 61½ Duke Street. Norman Manley had supplied us with an initial list of two thousand potential members, which he had compiled wharf by wharf before Busta's release. By the end of August, enrollment had surpassed four thousand and we had set up machinery to collect the weekly contributions of threepence from each enrolled member. The first entry in the Union cash book read:

> June 24 – By dues collected: £44. 0. 0; just over 3,500 paid up members. At the end of the first financial year – March 31, 1939 – paying membership stood at 6,500, with a balance sheet showing assets of £3,235. 0. 0

During the formative years of the Union we worked night and day, setting everything else aside, travelling the countryside, addressing meetings in the city and establishing a working Union office. I had never done this kind of work before.There were no precedents for a union of this size and type in Jamaica, and a lot of procedures had to be arrived at through trial and error.

My working day was from sun-up to sunset, with office work and public meetings all over the place. In a short time, I had become the principal day-to-day caretaker of what was the largest single organisation in Jamaica. The nearest to the BITU, in the number of members, would have been the Jamaica Agricultural Society but neither the JAS head office in Kingston nor any of its parish branches would ever be faced with the complex dealings that soon became commonplace for this new Union – workers' grievances, new members, strikes taking place with and without notice, calls for help from the countryside. In every case, it meant signing up more members and working out new strategies to bring about settlement and satisfaction.

After the offices were moved to 61 1/2 Duke Street, we began to recruit staff. We had to employ four young women, Miss E. Josephs, Miss Ivy Bailey, Miss Edith Nelson and Miss Olga Beckford, to act as cashiers and to attend to the registration of the large number of workers applying for membership. At that time the Executive of the Union consisted of Mr Bustamante, vice-presidents Mr H.M. Shirley and Mr Leslie Washington Rose, and Mr W.A. Williams and myself. Mr J.A.G. Edwards who had been assisting,was appointed to act as General Secretary, and when he left, Mr Penso filled the gap for a short time. After that, Mr Linden Newland was invited to join the team and he readily left his job at the Gleaner to do so. Soon he became General Secretary and eventually became the longest serving officer in that post. Others who filled that important niche during the earlier years of the Union, were Mr S.T. Morais, Miss Nelson, and organising officers Mr Vivian Durham and Mr G.S.L.Thompson,

We had a number of volunteers who came in as organisers, among them Mr Cyril Mallett who used to work on a temporary basis at the Myrtle Bank Hotel. He stayed with us for many years and was always a great asset to the movement. When he came along, our main organiser was St. William Grant who was travelling extensively throughout the country. We also had Mr Theophilus McPherson, the father of Mr Joe McPherson, who was put in charge of the office. I found out later that he also was from Westmoreland and that he used to hold me when I was a baby

The weight of the work was increasing rapidly, so I contacted Miss Marion Bravo, then employed to DeCordova Agencies, and asked if she would like to assist me. That was what she wanted to hear. It was she who had sent Edith Nelson to us and now she was glad to give notice to her employer and to become a part of the BITU. Up to this moment as I write she is still at the BITU, serving with the same devotion and commitment although over the age of seventy. Miss Nelson proved to be very reliable and it did not take long before she was made Assistant Secretary. Miss Beckford became chief cashier, a post from which she retired only a few years ago, due to ill-health. And there were other women who passed through the organisation, staying for differing lengths of time. Among them were Julia Griffiths, Myrtle Seivright, Pearl Jordan, Ivy Page, Phyllis Vassell, Conchita Corkery and Ena Mesquita, who would later become my personal secretary. It is certainly a mark of stability, good relations and satisfactory working conditions, that so many of the original recruits remained with the Union until their retirement.

We women were the mainstay of the Union's organisation, though we could hardly have functioned without the brave men who toiled day and night, facing all sorts of criticism and opposition as they tried to help the workers. Bustamante was the busiest of us all, scouring the rural areas, forming branches, listening to grievances, offering solutions and calling publicly upon Government as well as private employers to deal fairly with the masses. On nearly all these trips I was by his side, taking note of important details, seeing to his personal welfare and offering advice based upon my own experience, close contact with the people and, of course, a woman's intuition.

We had the solid support of the workers everywhere we went. Like many of us, they too were not familiar with trade unionism; and so Busta found it necessary to teach as well as to preach. He insisted on discipline, patience and understanding. He knew from observation abroad that if the workers went on strike without good reason their cause would be damaged. He advised them not to be impatient, not to expect too much in the short term and always to give the leaders time to build securely. He stood firmly against disorder and never failed to instil into the workers the need to use their union in a proper way. In his own words: "I should like the people to realise that if the unions are to be of assistance to them, they must bring all their grievances to be settled through negotiations conducted by Union officers on their behalf. For the Unions to succeed, they must have not only the respect of members but of all companies and other employers of labour."

This enlightened approach to worker-management relations was as sound as could be, but at every step there was opposition from employers and from the Government. At first the private sector, unaccustomed to dealing with organised labour and used to pushing the workers around, did not take the new union too seriously. At one point we were told that the shipping companies were planning a lock-out of workers if any unauthorised strike took place and that they would also be mechanising the loading and unloading of cargo. To this Bustamante responded:

> If the shipping companies can afford to close down their wharves for three months, I can get enough money to feed my Union members for six months. This talk of lock-out is sheer bluff; sheer propaganda . . . Workers in Jamaica are accustomed to starve. They cannot starve much more . . . However, let them, understand that not one of my Union members will starve.

Bustamante's style of talking back to employers and sternly telling the workers the way they ought to go, did not always go down well with his critics. Some began to call him a dictator, but in typical fashion he replied: "The other elements, the minority, have had their dictators for too long, then why should labour not now have a voice?" And when others began to question his motives, Norman Manley, his cousin, rose to his defence by saying, "Bustamante is Jamaica's labour leader by the only test that matters; and that is the confidence and the support of labour."

It was just as well that Mr Manley should have made those remarks, because opposition to Bustamante and the BITU was coming not only from the employers and the government. It was also being organised by others in the trade union field who may have been looking on with envy at the successes we were having where they had failed. Disturbances were fomented at nearly every public meeting that we held. A.G.S.Coombs (later popularly knwn as 'Father' Coombs) in particular was still upset at the rift that had developed when Busta resigned from his Jamaica Workers and Tradesmen Union. He had shifted his activities from Kingston to Montego Bay and from that point sought to agitate the workers in the western parishes, chiefly Westmoreland and St James.

The BITU team travelled to many parts of the country to carry out promotional and organisational work. Sometimes the warmth of our welcome was mixed with resentment demonstrated by a minority believed to have the encouragement and support of employers who feared the name Bustamante and did not want their workers unionised. On one such occasion, a gang of Mr Coombs's supporters tried to disturb our meeting in Montego Bay Square, an attempt which led to a widening of the differences between the then two unions. We had set up our platform on the balcony of the Court House and Bustamante was about to address one of the largest crowds ever assembled to hear him. Suddenly there was big commotion resulting from the crowd reacting to a group that had been booing, jeering and loudly expressing support for Coombs.

On Busta's instructions, I complained to the police officer in charge and asked him to do something to restore order. In those days, the police in each parish were led by an inspector sent out from England. In this case, the officer was Harvey Clarke who, like most of his colleagues, openly favoured the employers. He paid no attention to my pleas. When Bustamante saw what was happening, he shouted, "If Harvey Clarke is governor of this town, then I am king." The people loudly showed their approval, and when a section of the crowd angrily encircled the trouble-makers, the police quickly intervened and saved them from rough justice.

At a second meeting in the Square, Coombs himself appeared with his supporters beating drums and pans in a effort to confuse the gathering. As Bustamante began to speak, the noise intensified. He rushed from the platform and demanded that the police remove the hecklers or he would do the job himself. The crowd massed behind him and seemed ready to take matters into their own hands. Only then did the police order Coombs's men to disperse and they hurriedly took their exit with the police right behind them. After that, there was peace and good order. The BITU had established its foothold in the west and Coombs was in retreat.

Over in the east, the BITU got a good reception, largely because the troublesome element had been dealt with in an incident which had taken place even before the formation of the Union. We had gone to Port Antonio at the request of workers who had heard and read of Bustamante and his activities. Thousands had come by trucks, donkey carts, bicycles, on foot and by whatever means of transportation they could find. But others were determined to drive us out of town. They became boisterous and threatened to smash the platform that had been set up in front of the Court House. In fact, they did just that, throwing the pieces of the platform into the sea.

During the uproar, Busta called to a white man who had been pointed out to us as the senior officer in charge of the police in Portland. The man denied that he was a policeman and turned his back on us. At that point, a woman attending the meeting fell ill and, characteristically, Bustamante turned his attention to helping her. At a nearby bar where we went to get the woman a drink of ginger ale, we were confronted by a hostile group of men telling us to take the drink and leave the bar, the town and the parish. Bustamante took the bottle, paid for it and promised to return so that they could do whatever they thought they could do to him.

I pleaded with the Chief and begged him to ignore the men in the bar, but he insisted that I take care of the sick woman and leave him to do what he had to do. I was equally determined that he should not go back to the bar alone, so having asked some people to take the woman home, I followed Busta. In typical fashion he ordered a round of drinks for everyone, but they shouted, "You can't buy us with drink. We have all the drink we want."

Busta pulled himself up to his full height, shook his head and said, "Look at you all. You are naked and hungry. I wouldn't want to buy you. If your blasted bodies were being sold for a penny, I would not oblige you by paying a farthing!"

The men seemed stunned at his response to them. They were quiet as he turned and left the bar. But I did not like the look of things and advised him to call off the meeting and send the people home before any physical violence erupted. He followed my advice, but he said to the crowd, "I am leaving Port Antonio, but I will be back."

Ten months later, Busta was asked to return and this time the crowd came to escort us from as far off as Buff Bay. More and more people joined us as we went along and eventually we marched triumphantly into Port Antonio with the crowd singing and chanting,"We will follow Bustamante till we die." We had a wonderful meeting and launched a branch which was headed by Mr Leopold Lynch. One of the leaders of the disturbance at the first meeting, Reuben Gunter, was prominent among the greeters this time and he later became a supporter of the Union. He told us how he had been paid to make trouble and how sorry he was for what had happened.

In St Mary we had a similar case of rejection and return. Here too, the first encounter was before the advent of the BITU but this time it occurred after midnight on a Saturday in Port Maria. When we arrived in that town, Bustamante asked a policeman where we might get some refreshments. The officer told him that there was no place open at that time except the Port Maria Tennis Club where a dance was in progress. He felt certain that we would be accommodated there.

We found the club, went in and asked whether we could get some food and drink. We were told we could and Busta gave his order for four of us. However, as the waiter left us, we were approached by a tall, black man, Clifford Clemetson, who had been among the dancers. He spoke directly to Bustamante: "Are you Bustamante?"

The Chief replied, "Yes, I am. What ís wrong?"

Clemetson said angrily, "You are the man organising the niggers around here. You cannot drink in my club."

Busta was furious. He got up, met the waiter on his way with the drinks and turning to Clemetson, he said, "For your benefit, I am going to drink this and I am going to drink another and pay for it. This is my country, mister, and neither you nor anyone else can stop me going where I want, eat where I want, drink where I want, sleep where I want and visit where I want."

By this time, some of the dancers had gathered around to hear what was happening. One of them said, "Mr Bustamante should be allowed to have his drink." (This gentleman turned out to be the Resident Magistrate for St Mary, Mr Colin McGregor, who in later years became Chief Justice and was knighted by the Queen of England.) The more vocal in the crowd paid no heed to the magistrate and when some became boisterous, Bustamante made it clear to them that if they wanted to have "a Wild West show" they could have it by laying a finger on him.

After some argument, I persuaded Busta to leave but as we reached the exit a drunk with a bottle shuffled as if to strike the Chief. It was then that I summoned up the nerve to grab the offender by his tie and pull him to the floor. He was so frightened by my sudden move that he bawled out, "Take this mad woman off me!" We pushed him aside and went on our way to Kingston.

When the workers heard what had happened that night, they sent telegrams for Mr Bustamante to return to Port Maria for a public meeting. When the Union was formed, many of them joined up and Busta was able to get pay increases and improved working conditions in most places in Port Maria, including Clemetson's property. In fact, the episode had a happy ending, for Clemetson and Busta later became good friends and we did not have many meetings at Port Maria without Clemetson being there to support us.

The stress and strain of forming and building a trade union in 1938 was no easy burden to carry. Physical threats to our lives were one thing but in addition there were legal obstacles. Up to the time when the BITU was organised, few laws existed relating to the working classes. Those that did exist had remained essentially the same since the emancipation of the slaves, except for slight changess resulting from the Morant Bay uprising of 1865.

It was not until 1919 that a law was passed giving the workers the right to form unions and associations for the furtherance of their own interests. The Jamaican Trade Union Law of 1919 was modelled on the British Trade Union Law of 1871, but the clause permitting peaceful picketing was left out of the regulations meant for the Colonies. In fact, as the law stood a trade union could be held liable for any damage that might occur during a strike.

In December 1938, a new Trade Union Law was passed providing the framework for the modern development of unionism in Jamaica. It re-affirmed the workers' right to form a union, erased the obstacles of the previous period, protected the unions against liability for breach of contract in the event of a strike, prohibited legal action against a trade union for damages and initiated compulsory registration.

With the legal framework defined, the BITU pressed towards its basic aims as stated in its Rules of 1938. Two of these aims were:

> 1. To secure or assist in securing legislation for the protection of the Trade Union interests and general welfare of the workers.
>
> 2. To adopt any other legal method to secure equitable Old Age Insurance and other matter which may be decided upon as advisable in the general interest of the members, and be so

> declared by the Managing Executive Committee, or a majority of members present and voting at the Annual Assembly . . .

The BITU's programme for the workers was far more comprehensive than anything attempted by any of the unions that preceded it. The general upheavals of 1938 had led to the setting up of a Royal Commission, the Moyne Commission, later that year to enquire into the problems facing the country and this gave Bustamante an opportunity to present the Union's case with a Memorandum which we had worked out in consultation with the membership. Our proposals called for a minimum wage law, regulation of working hours, sick leave with pay for weekly and monthly paid employees, amendments to the Shop Assistants Law and other social measures. It is interesting to note the fanfare that attended the announcement of a Minimum Wage in the 1970s, yet it was the insistence of the BITU that gave Jamaica its first Minimum Wage Law on December 22, 1938. That law empowered the Governor in Privy Council to fix the minimum wage for workers in any industry or concern in which he was satisfied that the wages were unreasonably low.

The early achievements of the BITU were historic and far-reaching. Our agitation led to great changes in working conditions and provided the sturdy foundation on which the modern labour movement has been built. Not only did we hasten the passage of the Minimum Wage Bill, we also influenced progress in such vital areas as Workmen's Compensation. This Act was passed in 1937, but its application was severely limited. In fact, the largest category of workers – those engaged in agriculture – was excluded. It was therefore amended in 1939 and in later years became extended, including provisions for dependents.

Other early accomplishments included holidays with pay, introduced in 1947; the Factories Law of 1940 which replaced the obsolete Prevention of Accidents at Sugar Mills Law dating back to 1888; the Employment of Women's Law, passed in 1941, regulating the hours of work for female workers; updating of the Apprenticeship Law which had lain on the Statute Book since 1881; setting up of the Portworkers

(Superannuation Fund) Law, the Sugar Workers Pension Fund; and laws relating to slum clearance, the protection of dock workers, registration and protection of nurses; and the Trade Disputes Act of 1939 that provided for the mediation, conciliation and arbitration of disputes between employers and employees.

Underlying all this was what I regard as the Union's role as the great unifying force which Jamaica experienced with the formation of the BITU. The Union was the symbol and the rallying cry for united action among black people in Jamaica. Up to the upheavals of 1938, black people rarely pulled together in Jamaica. And never before in the history of Jamaica were so many Jamaicans seen pulling together as was seen from the first day that the Bustamante Industrial Trade Union came into being. Of course, this major event of 1938 was not the first time that that an attempt had been made to unite Jamaicans. Nor was it the first to meet with a measure of success.

There was never any problem in getting large numbers of Jamaicans to work together in churches, in Lodges, in Fraternal Societies such as the Jamaica Burial Scheme Society and the PORA (it started as the Prison Officers Relief Association and was later changed to People's Onward Relief Association). Jamaicans have pulled together in informal projects such as 'day for day' labour and 'Partner'; and they demonstrated an unusual togetherness in Marcus Garvey's Universal Negro Improvement Association. But nothing was ever witnessed up to 1938 that could equal the wave of solidarity with which the BITU was welcomed. And its coming marked the passage of the old order, never to be seen again.

8

Politics and Labour

VERY SOON AFTER THE TURBULENCE OF MAY 1938, more and more people were talking openly of a new Jamaica. There was a wide and enthusiastic search for different paths to the realisation of their hopes. Like Alexander Bustamante, I believe in first things first; so while some others in 1938 were primarily concerned with the broad question of self- government and dominion status for Jamaica, we of the BITU and those who believed in us were almost totally committed to everyday 'bread and butter' issues. In our view the urgent needs of the masses of Jamaicans were gainful occupation for the unemployed and better wages and conditions for those in work. True, these problems had been addressed before but never, in a hundred years, had there been any such opportunity to deal with them; nor was there such an iron resolve to get them settled to the satisfaction of the working classes.

It was our firm belief that hungry, discontented people would not be ready to assume responsibility for governing a country. There were those who argued that if only we could take the management of the country out of the hands of the British, the way would be open for enlightened planning and progress for the people. We too, believed in self-government, but we did not want to reach that goal by a scrambling short-cut which, without material and intellectual resources, could end in chaos, frustration and even further disappointment for the masses. Instead, we advocated as a first step a strong enlightened and healthy working and middle-class base upon which to build. We knew that this could only be achieved by satisfying the needs of the families and, in particular, the breadwinners.

Of course, we were not the only organisation to place priority on basic economic issues. Some old prejudices were slowly disappearing and as a new approach to labour-management relations took hold, persons in the higher income brackets, and even the more conservative institutions, were becoming more thoughtful of the actual suffering of the poor and the unemployed. This feeling was being expressed even in the Church. For instance, after a religious service at a chapel in Jones Pen, the Welsh-born head of the Methodist Church in Jamaica, the Reverend Armon Jones, was heard to say that when he looked at the congregation to whom he was preaching he felt that many of them were more in need of sixpence than of his sermon.

Not only was there talk of these needs: there was also action. As an example, the economic thrust of the Cooperative Movement was steadily gaining strength, mainly in the form of Credit Unions, promoted around the island by social workers of Jamaica Welfare. But it was the trade union movement that was in the forefront of the struggle for a better income, seeing this as the most immediate means to a better way of life.

Despite our firm convictions, we were willing to cooperate with any progressive organisation having a genuine commitment to the overall development of trade unionism and nation building. So when a national political movement was coming into being in September 1938, Bustamante was right there on the platform as one of the earliest supporters. As early as May 1938, Norman Manley had spoken of the need for a political party to work alongside a strong trade union movement, demanding self-determination for the Jamaican people as a whole. Four months later, the Peoples National Party was launched with an English guest speaker, the eminent barrister and parliamentarian, Sir Stafford Cripps, later to be Chancellor of the Exchequer in the British Labour Party after World War II.

Sir Stafford had travelled by sea to Jamaica with his two daughters. In order to avoid the newspaper reporters, the three were not registered in their real names on the passenger list. However, on the same ship was a young Jamaican doctor returning from his studies in England, and he struck up a friendship with Peggy, one of Sir Stafford's daughters. She confided the real identity of her father to him and also told him that the purpose of the visit was to speak at the inauguration of a political party. She told him the date of the Ward Theatre launching and invited him to be present. He did attend and later became a prominent member of the PNP. That young man was Dr Ken McNeill.

A sequel to the Cripps visit shows the dramatic changes in political and human relations that were taking place throughout the world in those times. Peggy Cripps went on to visit Africa and there she married a rising young African politician, Joe Appiah. Little fuss was made about this inter-racial marriage, and she worked for the independence of her adopted country which in 1957, as Ghana, would be the first black African country to gain independence from Britain. Among Jamaicans, the demand for a new Constitution, the activities of the Jamaica Progressive League and the formation of the PNP and the BITU constituted the awakening of a national movement that would result in independence in 1962.

In 1938, Jamaica's political leadership was taken up by Norman Manley. While recognising the importance of the labour movement, he correctly felt that a trade union could influence but not enact legislation and could not plan for wide-scale social and economic development. A political party was a necessity and this fact could, in 1938, be better recognised than it was a decade earlier when Marcus Garvey had formed the People's Political Party with a manifesto of far-reaching significance. Bustamante was fully in accord with the formation of the PNP. A few days before the launching of the party, he had met privately with Sir Stafford Cripps at Drumblair, the home of the Manleys. Because it was intended to have a labour movement going hand-in-hand with a political movement in Jamaica, so as to form a national movement, the original plan was that the new political party would be called the Jamaica Labour Party. In fact, just one day before the actual launching, a weekly newspaper came out with that announcement. But the seven-member task force in charge of the planning made a last-minute change. It was felt by the majority that in the circumstances of 1938, and since most Jamaicans were not familiar with political terms, the name *Labour Party* would almost certainly suggest that this would be a party solely or mainly for the working class. On the other hand, the words *National* and *People* could clearly be seen as all-embracing and, therefore, more appealing to the country as a whole. Thus, the PNP got its name. Incidentally, as I write, the sole surviving member of that task force is Sir Howard Cooke, the present Governor General of Jamaica.

A huge crowd gathered on September 18 for the meeting and the overflow from the Ward Theatre spilled onto North Parade and Victoria Park. People of all differing political persuasions were present and in his speech Mr Manley emphasised the need for coexistence and collaboration between politics and trade unionism. "My own position is perfectly clear," he said. "I have never pretended to be a labour leader and I have no ambition to be a labour leader. All I have offered is the counsel of a friend of the new labour movement in Jamaica. And so long as I have the power, so long as I maintain that position, so long as I enjoy that confidence, they will have my support, my help and my voice . . . .

"I want to tell you that, as far as I am concerned, I am not the author of this Party. I have discovered that a considerable number of persons in the country have been thinking about it, have been dreaming about it, but it wanted some convulsion to make it plain that such a thing was necessary . . . One thing that struck every thinking man in this country was the enormous growth of progressive ideas centring around the development of labour."

Following that meeting, the PNP began an islandwide campaign to organise political groups. The Kingston group was named the Metropolitan Group and Bustamante joined it. The Member of the Legislative Council for Kingston, the Hon. Erasmus Campbell, also joined but did not remain for long. When in 1944, under Adult Suffrage, he contested the East Kingston seat, it was won by a trade unionist, Florizel Glasspole.

However, Sir Arthur strongly supported the establishment of labour unions in Jamaica. Nevertheless, he was not happy with the flamboyant style and outspoken manner of Mr Bustamante. Sir Arthur must have considered him to be a veritable challenge to his will and wits. Their battles were frequent and often bitter, but in all of them, Busta never lost his self-possession.

In the earlier months of 1939, there were disturbances in Kingston, including a waterfront strike and the shutting down of the Constant Spring Hotel. The members of the Royal Commission which had come to the island at the end of 1938 were staying at the hotel at the time. It struck me as funny that they had their own taste of strike action in January and had to prepare their own meals until the staff resumed work. Then there was an incident in Montego Bay which led to Bustamante threatening to call an all-island strike. It did not materialise, largely because of the powerful concentration of forces opposed to him and to the BITU. The employers were fully mobilised to frustrate our efforts. Rival unions were doing all they could to defeat us and the Government, under Sir Arthur Richards, always there, determined to make life difficult for the man whom he had made his main target.

Repercussions from this incident resulted in more flagrant displays of employer antagonism to union representation. The Union had further trouble when waterfront workers in Port Antonio were persuaded to handle ships affected by strikes at Kingston wharves. Heartened by this, certain shippers made a concerted effort to break the Union by dismissing workers without just cause. A crisis was developing for the entire labour movement and it was at about this time that cooperation between the political and the trade union arms of the national movement seemed destined to work positively for both.

With Bustamante and Richards already at odds, Norman Manley, who enjoyed good relations with the Governor, offered to take over the role of mediator, just as he had done when Denham was in office. He requested the Governor to openly declare support for labour unions and also to let the employers know that he was against the growing practice of dismissing workers known to be unionised. Sir Arthur responded willingly, but laid down certain conditions which included the setting up of an advisory body for the guidance of all trade unions in the island. Busta agreed to this, but there was one other condition that he would not accept, and that was that the name of his Union should be changed.

The Governor was against any trade union being named after a single individual, but Busta had already gone through this with the workers and was determined to stand by their decision. When the Union was being formed, he had called a meeting at Kingston Race Course and it was suggested that the union be named after him. He said emphatically that he was not in favour of the suggestion but the crowd insisted and the deciding view was that the name of Bustamante would distinguish the union from the many that had been springing up and, in the general view, confusing and misleading the workers. Using his name would mean that those who joined would know exactly who was representing them.

When Manley told Sir Arthur that Bustamante did not favour the change, the Governor said he was no longer willing to give the public support requested. Manley then called Busta to come to his office and, in his presence, telephoned the Governor and appealed to him to let the name remain. Sir Arthur again said "No!" and Bustamante responded, "I will never agree to that. Never!" And he walked out of Manley's office. After that, Manley called the Governor yet again, telling him that if neither side would relent, the labour movement would be irreparably hurt. He was therefore asking him to reflect carefully on the matter and to call him back after he had done so. After some minutes, Manley reported, Sir Arthur called to say, "I have thought about it and I still think it is not right to have a labour union named after any man. It is against my better judgment, but I will agree to the request to help the union movement." He then issued a statement calling on employers to desist from efforts to stifle the workers' right to be unionised.

It was out of this understanding that a Trades Union (Advisory) Council was established,

> to rally all voluntary efforts on the part of persons willing to assist in the orderly and progressive development of the trade union movement, to prevent frivolous strikes, to unify policy, to eliminate strife amongst workers' organisations and between labour and capital and to pool all the labour resources for the common good.

We found this entirely agreeable in principle. Bustamante signified his approval at a meeting called by Manley at the Kingston Race Course on February 21 and the way was open for the development of the labour movement.

Mr Manley was the legal counsel for the twelve-member Trade Union Council and the Chairman was the solicitor N.N. Nethersole, then the leader of a number of small unions and a vice-president of the PNP. The other representatives included two from the Progressive League and two from the Conciliation Board, which Busta had previously described as nearly one hundred per cent capitalist. The BITU was offered three seats, making it a minority force in a Council that was said to be planning to take over from individual unions the negotiating of all major labour disputes and other matters affecting the welfare of the workers.

When news of this possibility began to spread, a number of members of the BITU insisted that Bustamante was the person they had chosen to represent them and that they would not be satisfied to have the Council act on their behalf. Some even went on to describe it as a plot to weaken Bustamante's position, but they agreed with our decision to wait and see how the TUC would conduct its affairs. However, other events and statements tended to cause us concern. We came to believe that our policies, our priorities and our path were decidedly different from those envisioned for the movement by other dominant elements. So we were in agreement to walk together but it seemed inevitable that, at a fork in the road, we would have to go our own way rather than dissipate our energies in argument and inter-union struggle.

The caution that we were practising and the suspicions we had harboured proved to be justified. A report made by Sir Stafford Cripps to the Secretary of State for the Colonies, Malcolm McDonald, revealed that while in Jamaica, helping to launch the PNP, Cripps had shown Bustamante a good face. Behind the mask, however, he was favouring Manley and quietly driving in his wedge. McDonald's report said:

> I had a talk yesterday with Sir Stafford Cripps about his visit to Jamaica. In the course of it, he told me that a very dangerous situation was arising around the figure of Bustamante . . .
>
> He is a thoroughly irresponsible agitator who does not know what his objectives are. He is organising a very powerful trade union which has no particular why or wherefore, except to strike every now and then for higher wages.
>
> Sir Stafford says that this cannot go on indefinitely. He tried to persuade Bustamante to have some responsible policy without success. Bustamante does not brook interference from anyone, and he has great power as an orator.
>
> However, Sir Stafford was inclined to think that in time the native people would discover their leader's defects and turn to others with more balance . . . Sir Stafford has a high opinion of Mr Manley and thinks that he will be able to form in Jamaica a reasonable labour movement. Manley . . . is deliberately keeping on good terms with Bustamante in order to retain his influence.

The BITU gradually withdrew from the TU(A)C and with the lapsing of Busta's membership in the PNP the division between us and the more politically inclined became pronounced. Thus were sown the seeds of Jamaica's two-party system – a divergence of thought which often led to acrimonious speech and action, when otherwise the situation might have gone on with respect between the rivals. For me, this bitterness between personalities and organisations was further proof that we as a people were not then sufficiently experienced nor quite ready to handle the complexities of state-craft and political self-determination.

It is not my wish to apportion blame for the schism which started then and persists to this day in Jamaica. It takes two or more to make a quarrel. However, from my vantage point, the flame of dissension was fanned by energetic activists who did not like Bustamante's style, were diametrically opposed to some of his policies and, sad to say, were scornful of the intellectual capacity of the workers and their chosen leaders. Some had got it into their heads that Bustamante was a semiliterate demagogue without the social and intellectual credentials for leadership. The time would come when they even campaigned against him on the grounds that he could not read or write and was therefore unfit to lead anyone who had benefited from schooling, had found acceptance in certain circles or who even wore a tie to work.

This business of class divisions and social snobbery in Jamaican politics was to follow us for a long time, but we learnt to take it in our stride rather than treat it as an obstacle to the effective pursuit of our mission. Yet I regret that up to now nothing worthwhile is being done to correct this fundamental flaw in our society. It is the result of our history. For generations, Jamaicans have grown up in a society divided by class and colour, and although conditions are not what they were in the thirties, it seems that it will take still more generations for those differences to become unimportant. Sixty years of observation and experience tells me that politicians will not succeed in changing the situation until they honestly recognise the historical roots of the problem and deal decisively with it.

When Bustamante first appeared at a street corner meeting, he was not immediately accepted because he was seen by the masses as one coming, not from a certain political party, but from a different class. Colour represented class in Jamaica and up to that moment no Jamaican of Bustamante's complexion had ever been seen at a street meeting making common cause with the poor and the oppressed, speaking openly on their behalf and loudly criticising the Governor and the Government. Once they recognised his sincerity and were convinced that he would not let them down, then an unbreakable bond was established.

Norman Manley was also faced with early distrust because he too was perceived as being from a different class. He was not white, but he was, in the eyes of the masses, a man holding retainers from big business, one of great intellect and independent means, living comfortably in upper St Andrew and having easy access to high society. No Jamaican with such credentials had ever before 1938 spoken or acted freely on behalf of the masses, so they looked suspiciously at his activities as a mediator. True, behind the scenes, he gave Bustamante considerable support, but outside he was perceived as one seeking to strike a balance between the workers and their employers at a time when the militant workers felt that 'he who is not with me is against me.' How different things might have been had Manley been seen more in the light of an uncompromising ally of Bustamante rather than a mediator.

To me Bustamante's goodwill and his wish for solidarity were never in doubt. I heard him tell a huge public meeting one night in 1940 with PNP stalwarts C.G. Walker and Samuel Marquis on his platform:

> I know this, that if Mr Manley cooperates with me as I will with him, that we will do something for this country. I will say this without any boast, that there is no greater power in this country than the combination of Manley and Bustamante. I intend to cooperate with the Party for the benefit of the masses. Any trouble that Manley and I may have in the future we will fight it out ourselves , , ,

In addition to the establishment of the Trades Union Council at the beginning of 1939, another body which was formed for the purpose of mediation was a Labour Department such as Bustamante had recommended at the BITU General Meeting that January.

With the Labour Department taking care of disputes, we were beginning to enjoy a respite from the hectic struggle. But things were never quite peaceful, for the workers were often restive, dissatisfied and eager to use the one weapon they had – the withholding of their labour. This caused Bustamante to chide the workers on a number of occasions, declaring that unauthorised work stoppages would do more harm than good for the Union. We were constantly trying to maintain peace and promote the orderly settlement of differences. However, certain employers seemed to make it their business to provoke and test the temper of the workers by using the old strategy of divide and rule.

One Sunday morning in June, there was an outburst which resulted from rivalry between the BITU and a new body of wharf workers. Made up mostly of ex-servicemen, they had been encouraged by the employers and were organised by a World War veteran, H.M. Reid. It appeared that they had been getting some preferential treatment over the established port workers who objected to what they saw as a threat to the united front that they had been showing the shippers.

Reid's men were being escorted to the wharves by a separate truck carrying armed policemen when some stone-throwing began. A man who was seen to raise his hand in the act of throwing was fired upon by the police and died on the spot, the bullet passing through his chest and entering the southern wall of the Gleaner Company's building on Port Royal Street.

The BITU had not organised or sanctioned this protest, but when it was ascertained that the dead man was a member of our union, Bustamante went down to the waterfront and was shown a portion of the man's flesh lying on the roadside after the body had been removed. The Gleaner reported next day that Bustamante, in the presence of a quiet group of his followers, took out his handkerchief, wrapped the piece of flesh in it and told the workers who had gathered to go to Kingston Race Course for a meeting with him later that day.

It was surmised that Busta's reaction was a mixture of respect for the dead and cold anger at the wanton slaying of a human being. He was quiet and pensive that morning, but even as he mused upon the event, a group with no known dispute began to attack shops from downtown up to Constant Spring,, looting groceries and assaulting anyone who stood in their way. Governor Richards rapidly proclaimed a State of Emergency and this meant that the Race Course meeting could not be held.

The Governor's States of Emergency as well as the Labour Department's conciliation efforts did bring a measure of peace on the trade union front. Wildcat strikes were fewer and, where genuine disputes arose, the workers were more inclined to wait on due process.

The winding-down of union activity in the second half of 1939 was accelerated by the threat of war in Europe where Adolph Hitler's Nazi Germany was making aggressive moves to expand its territory. After September 3, when Britain declared war against Germany, union activity almost came to a stop for a considerable time. The war effort became the main concern and it would remain so for another five to six years. During those years Jamaicans realised, as never before, that the artificial divisions of the world made little difference to reality and that each part of the world bore some relationship to the other. On distant battlefronts, Jamaican volunteers were fighting and dying and, here at home, wartime constraints dug deeply into the comforts of our accustomed ways of daily life.

9

World War II

IN THE FIRST MONTHS OF THE WAR, there was little immediate threat of danger in this part of the world and few of us could foresee the hardships there would be for Jamaica, so far away from the major battlefields. There was recruiting for the armed services and men and women volunteered, as they would throughout the war. We now had a local radio station, ZQI, and to boost our patriotism and loyalty to the Mother Country, it played Land of Hope and Glory every afternoon at the beginning of broadcasting.

However, preparations were being made to maintain peace and quiet within the country. World War II took all of us in Jamaica into a permanent State of Emergency under Wartime Emergency Regulations, as it did in British territories around the world and in the UK itself. The State of Emergency meant that limitations were set on the holding of public meetings and on the size of meetings that were held. Any activity which might be considered to be a threat to law and order was forbidden and an internment centre was set up in Up Park Camp. Resident aliens, that is, any citizens of Germany, Italy or any other country with which Britain might be at war, and anyone else who might be considered to be a threat to the war effort, were taken from their homes and housed there, supposedly 'for the duration', of the war. And rationing of scarce commodities was introduced.

Since so many of the things we relied upon, including food, were imported, the country was at the mercy of external conditions. Commonly used everyday commodities were either rationed or not available at all. There was little we could do about the short supply of gasoline, kerosene, butter, cloth or paper. The newsprint on which the Gleaner was printed was so scarce that the size of the daily issue had to be drastically reduced and then it would be recycled as wrapping paper for groceries or even as bathroom tissue.

Usually in times of shortages and difficulties, there are some persons who are more privileged than others. However, when the worldwide restrictions of a major war pressed on Jamaica, most people fared alike. Petrol was in such short supply that it was issued only to essential services, including doctors. The trams were still running in Kingston, but the load of passengers made it almost impossible to get a 'cotch' even on the steps, so it was not unusual to see individuals accustomed to driving their own cars being driven in a buggy instead or enjoying a ride in a donkey cart. Some of the less affluent, used to walking from downtown to Constant Spring and beyond, didn't mind the journeying but there were others who had to nurse aching feet and backs until they became accustomed to the unfamiliar exercise.

A very large percentage of Jamaicans had their darkness lit by kerosene lamps, but as this fuel was also in short supply, ways and means had to be found to brighten the corners of the house. I am still grateful to a country woman who showed me how to thread a piece of twine through a hole made in some light material, thus getting it to float in a small tin of coconut oil. The twine could then be lighted as a wick and made a substitute for a lamp. I also learnt how to use a razor blade to cut down the length of a matchstick in order to get more than one strike from a single match.

It was not only homes that were often plunged into darkness through lack of coal for the Public Service generators or the shortage of kerosene. The Emergency Regulations dictated that no lights were to be seen from the outside of any house because of the possibility of an air raid, in which case a light would aid the enemy. This risk was made a little more likely by the fact that a United States air base was located at Vernam Field in Clarendon. It had a naval counterpart at a nearby islet known as Goat Island, and the US Navy officially designated it a warship — the USS Goat Island. The British had their own Naval Intelligence Unit stationed at Port Royal.

An islandwide campaign, with prizes offered, was run under the title Food for Family Fitness (3F) to encourage people to devise satisfying meals with the limited foodstuffs that were available. A man from Glengoffe, St Catherine, came up with an unusual idea. His menu was: Cut one cho-cho into two halves. Put one half in the centre of the plate and call it 'food'. Then put the other half at the side of the plate and call it 'fish'. I agree that it did not deserve a prize, but it certainly indicated how desperate conditions were. One kind of food that was never in short supply, since it could no longer be exported, was bananas. These appeared in every possible shape and form until people were weary of them.

As months of war turned into years with no end in sight, serious Jamaicans felt that, war or no war, neither the labour movement nor the political movement could be put on hold indefinitely. Union organising went ahead and political meetings were well-attended at Edelweiss Park, which used to be the home of Marcus Garvey's UNIA. Afterwards it became the headquarters of O.T. Fairclough's *Public Opinion* and also of the People's National Party. Fairclough had leased the place with option to purchase and years later the proceeds of the sale of the option enabled him to buy a new home for the paper and the City Printery at Torrington Road. That road was and still is the boundary between Kingston and St Andrew. If you occupied premises on the southern side you would be in Kingston; and if you were on the northern side you would be in St Andrew. I used to go from parish to parish because my dressmaker, Mrs Livingston, did her sewing on the St Andrew side and my friend, Mr Hylton, the shoemaker and daddy of Alma, lived and kept his business on the Kingston side.

On the waterfront, shipping for civilian and trade purposes was severely restricted. Most ships had been commandeered for military transport, and in any case, few and far between were the civilians who had any desire to be anywhere on the high seas. German U-boats were sinking vessels on all the oceans and the disruption of shipping left Jamaica unable to export its main crop – bananas. The result was greatly reduced employment; and with more dogs than bones, rivalry among job-seekers intensified. It was then that there was a real tug-o'-war between members of the BITU and those of H.M. Reid's union.

Most of the BITU men were of the view that it was their union that had brought improvements in the conditions on the waterfront and that any other union was superfluous. They wanted to continue speaking with one voice, since it was obvious that the redresses of 1938 would not satisfy all future circumstances and that fresh demands would have to be made. However, as there was no closed shop, the employers used their power to divide the work between the two unions, thereby maintaining the rivalry between them and undermining the possibility of their uniting to promote the best interests of both sets of workers.

On the night of September 7, 1940, the BITU workers, having failed to reach an amicable understanding with Reid's union members, crowded into the old 'Conversorium', the Central Branch school premises on Church Street, to make a public complaint about the splitting of the labour movement on the waterfront. Bustamante agreed with their stand, for he felt that a great wrong was being done by those who sought to shatter the solidarity so necessary in the struggle against the might of the establishment. He saw it as an act of betrayal and he was furious as he spoke about it. Never have I seen him so upset and never, I think, did he ever speak with greater passion. At one point, this man, who had so often preached respect for law and order in all battles, was so moved that he said, "I have stood for peace from the first day I have been in public life, but my patience is exhausted. This time, if need be, there will be blood from the ramparts to the grave."

The Governor was being supplied by an efficient intelligence machinery with up to the minute information on all developments which could be classified as being damaging to the war effort. Shortly after the meeting at the Conversorium ended, Richards was in possession of a report on the meeting. Early the next day, without warning and without a charge, Richards ordered that Bustamante be interned under the Defence of the Realm Act, meaning that he was considered a threat to the war effort. It all seemed so ironic, because at that very Conversorium meeting-place less than five months before, Bustamante had told cheering thousands, "It is better to have England with all her faults for one hundred years than to have German rule for one day . . . . In this time of trouble I shall never become a traitor to Great Britain. . . Tonight, I say from my heart that I am prepared, if it becomes necessary, not only to fight for England, but to die for her."

After Bustamante's arrest, there were numerous strikes, protest marches, cane fires and other forms of demonstration throughout the island. I used to visit him as often as possible, and on one of those visits, he gave me a message for the people. He told them that they should remain calm and not do anything to endanger themselves or the Union. Other officers of the BITU were also advised not to cause or encourage disruptions, as this would not be helpful. The people argued that their leader had done no wrong and that it was a grave injustice to lock him away. They were adamant and when things got hot, Busta was approached by the Security Forces and asked to send out a letter which would be read to the people around the country. He did just that and some peace was restored. In the calm that followed, the people got together with officers of the Union and recommended that a petition for Bustamante's release be sent to the Secretary of State for the Colonies in England. This was done.

Stout hearts kept both labour and the political movements alive. But for public meetings, we, like everyone else, had to get a permit. We also had to be very careful what was said on the platform or within earshot of the police note-takers. In fact, people were well advised to exercise caution in speaking anywhere at all. One of the *Gleaner*'s writers, Gordon St C.Scotter, an Englishman who had been a Police Inspector, found himself in the wartime internment centre because of remarks he had made in a bar. Scotter, who had a more than ordinary fondness for a sip, was known to speak his mind strongly after a bit of conviviality. On one occasion, he stated his objection to the increasing number of American service men in this British colony, and since such remarks were considered offensive by the authorities, he was taken into custody.

Ironically, Scotter was very anti-labour. Once, in 1938, he wrote an article questioning Bustamamante's motives in acting on behalf of the workers. He had asked: 'What is at the back of Bustamante's mind? What are his personal motives? Are they purely altruistic? Does he do what he does simply for the people alone? Are they pecuniary? Is any-money he may be paid for his labours the motive? Is it personal, that most fatal of all temptations to the strong?' Bustamante had replied strongly: 'Yes, I want power to be able to defend those weaker than I am .... The voice of labour must be heard and it shall be heard through me, whether Scotter and his frightened few like it or not . . .'

What a coincidence! Both ending up the the same detention centre. I recall Busta saying to me one day when I went to see him, "Just look who is my neighbour!" And there was Scotter in the little house next to the one that Busta occupied. I remember that at one time Mr B. was keeping a goat in the small yard at the back to supply him with milk. Scotter didn't stay in Camp for long, but many months passed while Bustamante languished in detention. Then, in 1941, Mr George Hall, Under-Secretary of State for the Colonies, visited Jamaica and went to see Bustamante. He told the Chief that the Colonial Office had received the petition and added that he could not do anything in Jamaica. However, he intended to deal fairly with the case when he returned to London. After a couple of months, Bustamante was told that his imprisonment would be suspended on certain conditions. These included:

> a) . . . Alexander Bustamante shall not address, or be present at, any open-air meeting, gathering or assembly of persons, march or procession, of any kind whatsoever, except . . . as a spectator at any bona fide race meeting or athletic or other sporting contest.

> b) . . . Alexander Bustamante shall not address, or be present at, any indoor meeting, gathering or assembly of persons, of any kind whatsoever, if more than fifty persons (including himself) are present except . . . (i) as a member of the congregation at any religious service held under the authority of the heads of denomination set out in the Schedule . . . (ii) as a member of the audience at any bona fide cinematograph, musical or theatrical entertainment.

The schedule went on to provide that if on any occasion Busta was permitted to speak at any function, ' . . . no broadcast or other sound reproduction or recording' should be made of any words spoken by him. In addition, he was required to submit to censorship, all matter ' . . . composed, supplied or written . . .for publication in any newspaper or periodical . . .and shall not publish or cause or permit to be published, any such matter save with the written consent of, and in the form approved in writing, by such authority.'

Bustamante was further required to state the address to which he was proceeding from prison and ' . . . if at any time thereafter the said Alexander Bustamante proposes to reside at any other address, he shall first himself inform the officer in charge of the Central Police Station, Sutton Street, Kingston . . .' On top of that, he was not to leave the Corporate Area for any purpose without giving the police prior notice of his destination.

The terms of his release were conveyed to Bustamante in a letter from Mr. J. Lucie Smith, Acting Colonial Secretary. He was asked to state whether he fully understood the conditions. Upon his affirmative response, he was taken from the detention centre to King's House to see Sir Arthur Richards. I went with Busta that morning and, in my presence, Bustamante told the Governor that, while he would respect the terms of his release, he would continue to fight for the cause to which he had dedicated himself. He said that nothing would deter him; and he let Richards know that in his opinion that those who had the authority to investigate his detention and did not do so, were dishonest and that he would see to it that such persons were made to leave the country.

Some months after, the Kingston and St Andrew Corporation Council arranged a send-off for the Governor who was scheduled to leave for a post in Nigeria, and Busta was invited. He refused to attend, replying, "I would rather hear of his Excellency's absence." Yet Bustamante did not harbour any malice toward his captors. His reconciliation with Sir Arthur Richards (later Lord Milverton) is well known.

The then Colonial Secretary, Mr Grantham, left the island in 1941 while Busta was still interned, but before leaving he wrote the following letter to him:

> Dear Mr. Bustamante,
>
> It was a real pleasure to receive a letter from you congratulating me on my promotion to Nigeria, and I reciprocate your remark regarding our mutual regard and friendship, for although we may have had disagreements in the past, I have never felt anything approaching enmity towards you; in fact it has been difficult to disagree with you because I have always liked you so much.
>
> I am truly sorry to leave Jamaica at this present time, when so many things of importance are happening. I only trust that everything will come out for the best in this lovely, but disturbed island of ours — (Now that I am leaving, I suppose I should say 'yours'.)
>
> With kindest regards and every good wish.
>
> Yours very sincerely,

A week later, Mr Grantham, while aboard his departing ship, wrote the following to me

> Dear Miss Longbridge,
>
> My wife and I were very touched with the bouquet of flowers that you and Mr. Bustamante so kindly gave us. Thank you both very much indeed. I feel that it was 'a gift from the heart,' for, as no doubt you know, Mr. Bustamante and I may differ so far as our heads are concerned, but not as regards our hearts. I received a very nice letter from him, just after my promotion had been announced.
>
> When next you see him, please give him my kindest regards.
>
> Yours sincerely,

The exchange of letters between the two antagonists is typical of Bustamante's undying sense of forgiveness and accommodation. He was at times an angry man, a determined man speaking his mind with forthrightness, but I have never known him to hate or despise anyone. It is remarkable that even those who cursed his name and tried to devalue his deeds often ended up happily in his company. He was one who always offered the hand of peace, friendship and reconciliation; and even comfort and assistance to a fallen foe. Yet the most virulent attacks against him were more often directed at his personality rather than his principles. This strategy, when practised by political leaders, tends to be copied by followers who in turn treat their opponents with the same intolerance and disrespect

An important episode that further demonstrates the Jamaican tendency to split movements took place while Bustamante was in detention. It also shows some of the early trends that led to the break between the PNP and the Bustamante forces although it developed from a good , but now questionable, intention. Norman Manley had offered his services to help keep the Union vibrant during Busta's incarceration. The Chief agreed, instructing that in his absence, H.M. Shirley, the BITU Vice-President, would be in charge, with Samuel Morais, a waterfront delegate, as Secretary, myself as Treasurer and Edith Nelson as Assistant Secretary.

In his effort to assist, Mr Manley selected some of his most effective party organisers and brought them into the BITU to work with us. These men included Ken Hill, who had earlier resigned from the Union, the President of the TU(A)C, N.N. Nethersole, Frank Hill, Richard Hart, Arthur Henry, Roy Woodham, Osmond Dyce, Ken Sterling and Winston Grubb. We were glad to have the help of such energetic and capable people. However, from the very start, they seemed determined to change the organisation to suit their own outlook rather than that of Bustamante. H.M.Shirley, a nice but weak man, was a railway worker who had obtained leave from his workplace to help the Union. He did good work, but unfortunately was persuaded to establish official links with the TU(A)C and gradually became a willing tool of his new-found friends.

Manley himself made regular reports to Busta, but I don't think he quite understood what his colleagues were trying to do. I believe he expected them to concentrate on field work, but they were anxious to make fundamental changes, without consultation with or agreement from Bustamante. Word began to be spread that Bustamante was not the right sort to lead the Union, that he was dictatorial and that the Constitution of the BITU gave him too much power. The new men began to raise questions about the organisation's finances and Mr O'Brien, the auditor left by Bustamante, was replaced by Gerald Mair and Company, a firm appointed by them.

Meanwhile, we Bustamante loyalists, including myself, L.W. Rose, Edith Nelson, W.A. Williams, Cyril Mallett, 'Doc' Newland and Theophilus McPherson, were being isolated and sometimes ignored. One morning I arrived to find the new auditors waiting for me. They gave me instructions to open the safe and hand over books and cash to them. The detractors were smiling, but I had the last laugh when after all the auditing had been completed they had found four shillings and sixpence in excess of what should have been in the accounts. Furthermore, the accounts prepared by the auditors were rejected by the Registrar-General because their appointment had not been approved by the Colonial Secretary.

I felt that what was going on was wrong, that any change should await Bustamante's return and that genuine helpers would not be so busily engaged in furthering their own ends. However, on my frequent visits to the detention centre, I kept Bustamante completely abreast of what was happening but I played down some of it, just to ensure his peace of mind. Still, we, his supporters, were not prepared to see his work destroyed by seeming friends and secret foes.

In addition to the wartime conditions, gossip, undermining and rumour-mongering were affecting the Union membership and its finances. Many of the workers objected to the activities of the new-comers and their interest in the organisation declined, particularly as their chosen leader was not present.. Matters came to a head when a meeting was arranged for Monday, February 9, 1942, to change the Constitution so that Bustamante could no longer be President-General for life. As it happened, Bustamante's release was impending, but I did not tell the plotters of my visit to King's House on Saturday the 7th. So when Bustamante suddenly appeared at the BITU office on Sunday, the day of his release, those present were dumbfounded. They quickly contacted their colleagues and the planned meeting was postponed.

Some days later, when Bustamante decided to go to the office, he found his detractors in a militant mood. They wanted to have it out with him and when he invited them to sit and state their grievances, they retorted that they wanted to have nothing to do with any dictator. "We want democracy in this Union!" they shouted.

Bustamante replied, "I want you all to understand that this organisation was built on my blood and the suffering of the workers. . . you will not be allowed to smash it." Then, pointing at them individually, he said, "Shirley, you are fired! Morais, you are fired! Hamilton, you are fired! McBean, you are fired! Chambers, you are fired! Nelson, you are fired!" And, in chorus, they declared, "You can't fire we! More than one coffin will come out of here today." At that point, the Chief rose to his full height, grabbed a chair and began swinging it at them. The chair broke on one of their backs and they all fled the room, never to return to 61 1/2 Duke Street.

Shortly after that incident, a crowd of workers came to the Union Hall to find out what had happened. They said they had long suspected that something wrong was going on and that Busta should have called them to deal with the trouble-makers. Busta told them not to mind as he had already dealt effectively with the matter. In fact, he was made to pay a fine of ten pounds in court when some of those who had been driven from the office, reported him for assault and battery.

The upshot of this confrontation was that Bustamante angrily denounced what he described as "an unholy combination of persons with political ambition whose objective is that of destroying me and then to assume control of the Union as a political machine . . ." Manley responded by going to the aid of those he had sent to the BITU. He said it was time to break with Bustamante, and he levelled a number of accusations against him, including ingratitude, incompetence and financial mismanagement. He also stated that Bustamante had made a deal to attack the PNP in exchange for his freedom. Of course, nothing of the kind had happened.

Busta's response to the attack was to reorganise the executive of the Union and pull further away from Manley, the PNP and the TU(A)C. Shirley tried to form a union of his own and Manley welcomed it into the TU(A)C. However, Shirley's attempt failed and while the anti-Bustamante faction wallowed in the misery of their own making, the workers called a huge meeting at the Ward Theatre on March 31, 1942, to reaffirm their faith in Bustamante as hero and saviour of the working classes. They sang, 'We Shall follow Bustamante till We Die', the song that had been written and composed by Edgar Hall of Portland back in the days when we were making the triumphant return to Port Antonio. The jubilant workers chanted, "Shirley gone, Shirley gone, Shirley gone to a silent home, And forever with Manley, Amen so let it be." Then they symbolically buried the two. And so, the rift widened. With each utterance from either side, positions hardened and it was as if everyone had agreed never to agree.

PAN AM
EXPERIENCED
PAN AM

10

Party Politics

ONCE BUSTAMANTE HAD RETURNED to active unionism and the disruptive elements had been removed from the BITU, there was a period of calm in which the administration was put on stronger footing. Out in the field, the Chief was visible and vocal. Moreover, he was assisted by a team of committed organisers, concerned with helping the workers.

With the resurgence, membership that had been dwindling because of internal conflict and restrictions imposed by wartime conditions, began to grow again. Not only were the numbers increasing, but the spirit of the workers was also being revived, largely due to the grassroots organising and the hard work of the branch secretaries around the island. Among them were men such as Barnes, Isaac Barrant and John Barrett in St Thomas, Leopold Lynch in Portland and John Regeorge Henry of Brown's Hall in St Catherine.

Within a year of Busta's return, and with the trouble-makers out of the way, the Union was able to purchase for cash its new headquarters at 98 and 100 Duke Street. Number 98 had been an old guest house operated by a Mrs Prendergast and number 100 was a vacant lot. This acquisition of valuable real estate was a signal of the strength and independence of the organisation. The workers were very proud of the achievement and so were the officers. It was the first time that any union had become owner of its own property and the BITU had done this in less than five years. We remained at this location in the old guest house until 1962-1963 when the new head office was constructed. The Union's large, imposing building and the additional real estate it owns on Duke Street should answer those jealous critics who used to make wild accusations about the so-called mismanagement of union funds.

One member of the new working team at headquarters was a young accountant, St Clair Shirley, who rose to become an executive of the Union and later an officer of the Jamaica Labour Party and member of Parliament for West Portland. Another very enthusiastic young man was brought into the Union by L.G.'Doc' Newland. He had joined the staff just after leaving school and was at first assigned to helping produce the organisation's newspaper, *The Jamaica Worker*. I remember one occasion when I took a copy of the paper to Busta in detention, he began reading an article on the front page.

"Who wrote this?" he asked, knitting his brow. I tried to brush the matter aside and replied, off-handedly, "Oh, it is only a little youngster who has just started with the Union."

But Busta kept on the subject. "How much do you pay him for this work?"

"Ten shillings a week," I replied.

To this Busta responded, "Give him sixteen shillings. I can see something in him." And he chuckled.

The young writer was Hugh Shearer who rose to become not only a first-class trade unionist but an outstanding legislator and Prime Minister as well. I don't think any other labour organisation can claim to have nurtured an individual from his earliest working days to the highest political office in the country. This was a direct result of the mutual confidence, respect and understanding that existed between Bustamante and Shearer. Temperamentally, they were poles apart; in age they had a great generation gap, but Hugh was always an apt student, a loyal colleague and a faithful friend. No one ever wondered at all that he was, without question, the natural successor to Bustamante both in the Union and in the political party.

Although we have never discussed it in depth, I have always felt that Hugh was far more comfortable with union work than he was with politics. I think he liked politics only a little more than I did. Yet, when duty called and his leader needed him, he never hesitated to give to his task the energy and full devotion that it deserved. I consider it a pity that the outstanding accomplishments of his term as Prime Minister of Jamaica seem to have sunk in a sea of forgetfulness.

It was in 1942, after his release, that Bustamante announced his inclination to form a political party. He had discussed the idea with me and others close to him, for he was feeling, even then, that the activities of the PNP and its declared socialistic tendencies were inadvisable. He believed in free enterprise and the PNP did not. Although he had supported the party at the beginning when it was said to be a national movement, he was never happy with it after Norman Manley, addressing the Annual Conference in 1940, declared, "Socialism is not a matter of higher wages or better living conditions for workers, though these things are important, but it involves the concept that all the means of production should, in one form or another, become to be publicly owned and publicly controlled."

We sensed that there had to be an alternative to this but the urgency of Union affairs caused political matters to be placed on the back burner. Then, in January 1943, when a delegation including Manley and Members of the Legislative Council was named to go to London for discussions on the fom the new Constitution should take, Bustamante was left out. He felt that this was because he was being regarded as a labour leader rather than as a national leader and that irked him. He had me send a telegram to the Government, which read: *All the Elected Members combined don't represent even five per cent of population or views of this country. Manley represents . . . negligible minority*. It is perhaps worth noting here that the need to agree on and introduce a new Constitution for Jamaica was considered by the British Government to be so urgent that, even in the middle of a world war, the preparatory meetings were being held in London.

In July the new party was formed and, as some of its critics were anxious to say, it resembled not much more than the BITU with a political label. That did not bother any of us, for we had long been aware that the Chief's immediate concern was the upliftment of the workers through improvements to their social and economic conditions. In fact, the demands of the leading activists of the BITU and the main planks of the political party included worker-oriented programmes such as old age pensions; an eight-hour day for all workers; minimum wage for all; workmen's compensation; and State aid for poor expectant mothers. Also included were measures for more land settlement schemes, legal aid for persons unable to afford it and medical examination of prisoners to determine their fitness to serve sentences.

When it came to naming the party, the matter was a simple one. Busta told his close colleagues that he wanted two words in the name – *Jamaica* and *Labour*. Someone said, "Then call it Jamaica Labour Party." And so it was that the same name that the PNP had rejected became the banner of the workers' political movement. Under this flag. some of the country's humblest citizens would rise to prominence as representatives of their community and their country. Predictably, they would be treated with scorn by certain intellectuals and their supporters, but such acts would serve only to widen the divisions in the society

The first slate of candidates named was hurriedly put together to meet the first elections under Adult Suffrage. The new Constitution established a House of Representatives in which all the seats would be held by elected members. There would also be a Legislative Council and an Executive Council. Voting was to take place on November 20, less than eighteen months after the launching of the JLP.

We would be running against a party that had been in the field busily organising for more than five years and had, in addition to a band of competent organisers, the open support of some very well-known public figures. We would also be up against a third force, the Jamaica Democratic Party, formed before the JLP and representing the views of the employer class – pen-keepers, land-owners and merchants. Many of these had favoured the national movement but had backed off when the socialist tag became attached to the PNP.

In the run-up to the election campaign, some observers were talking about a fight between the PNP and the JDP. The JLP was not given much notice because we were considered to be without political experience at the leadership level, merely a bunch of unsophistcated spokesmen and a one-man show that would not be accepted outside union circles. One instance of our supposed innocence was that the Chief had been nominated as Alexander Bustamante although his name had not been officially changed from Alexander Clarke. This would have cost him his seat and moves were being made to defeat him on that ground. However, we got wind of the plan and the matter was regularised by deed poll in time.

JLP candidates represented a wide spectrum of the society. We had men from the schoolroom, from the farms, from the trade union, from business and from the legal profession. And we also had a woman, the first one to be elected to the House of Representatives – Iris Collins of St James. She had been an ardent community worker and an elected member of the Parochial Board, the then equivalent of the Parish Council.

When we nominated Isaac Barrant for Eastern St Thomas, we were laughed at because he was of humble birth, with little formal education and an occupation considered by snobs to be beneath the dignity of Parliament. However, he won by an overwhelming majority. He served well and justified Bustamante's faith in the potential of people from the masses. Busta's defence of the 'small people' was a serious matter. He would tolerate a joke against himself but he never permitted one to be made based on the former station in life of any of his candidates.

Barrant had been compelled to leave school when his father died and he had to support the family and he turned his hand to anything he could find. He worked as a labourer's headman on parochial roads and as a linesman on sugar estates. He helped to load trucks, tried small farming and shop-keeping, anything to make an honest living. And he used his 'gift of the gab' to help the people he worked with.

He joined the BITU in the early days and soon became an energetic organiser of the Union in St Thomas. He did very well and when the time came for the selection of candidates for the 1944 elections few, if any, had a better claim to loyalty and willingness to sacrifice for the working people. He knew the meaning of 'hard life' and the hunger of the poor and the obstacles they faced in struggling for betterment. He could speak and think clearly, he had a vision and the energy to make plans work and he had proven his worth through union representation. What more could we ask of a candidate?

Nowadays, in electoral matters, we tend to put our trust only in college graduates and men of letters, forgetting that among the so-called uneducated there are some who have a valuable role to play. Academic excellence does not necessarily produce the best leaders or the greater number of new ideas or the faithfulness and fearlessness required in the struggle to move forward. Leadership is needed at all levels of the society. Those such as Bustamante and Barrant are blessed with certain inborn qualities that will emerge once opportunity is allowed to flow freely throughout the society.

Isaac Barrant's life is a fitting example of what I mean. He owned no farm or large estate. He had never travelled far beyond his native parish yet, before he died at the early age of forty-six, he had become perhaps the best Minister of Agriculture the country ever had. He was ridiculed in the press but he rose proudly above the scorn. I remember that in the early fifties he tried might and main to convince the colonial officials who dominated the Executive Council that they should launch a programme of soya-bean cultivation to produce milk, cereal, oil and other by-products. Nobody among the wise men in authority would listen. Many years later, Jamaica came around to the idea and still we have been so half-hearted about it that the country is now importing large quantities of soya products. What if Jamaica had shared Barrant's vision? And it was he who first invited Jamaica's hoteliers to work with Jamaican farmers to produce food for tourists.

There were other earthy JLP candidates in that first election under Adult Suffrage. Leslie Washington Rose, a shoemaker and son of a watchman; Leopold Lynch, a tailor from Buff Bay, who campaigned on a bicycle; and John Regeorge Henry, a small cultivator and union officer from St Catherine. All three won their seats convincingly.

Although we were mocked for the supposed quality of some of those chosen to contest a seat, the JLP had been very careful in the selection of candidates in that first general election. I don't think that we had one who had not previously given satisfactory service and shown leadership either in their community or their profession. The overall victory of the JLP in 1944 vindicated Busta's correct reading of the will of the people. Also, the stated objectives of the Party coincided exactly with the desires of the broad mass of voters while those who had their own ideas of what was good for the people had their programme decisively rejected. The JLP took 22 of the 32 seats, Independents gained 5 and the PNP ended up with 5, including the Eastern Westmoreland seat won by an Independent, F.L.B.Evans, who switched to the PNP on the day that Parliament was convened.

Fred Evans was a maverick politician and it was against him that I was nominated on the only occasion that I got involved in active politics. He had won his first seat by riding a donkey and meeting villagers in their homes. He held no public meeting and selected certain strategic areas in which to campaign and use his powers of persuasion. He won handsomely and turned out to be one of the colourful characters in representative politics. He was always at odds with the Speaker of the House and once brought Parliament to a standstill by grabbing the Mace from the table and running outside with it. No Mace, no meeting.

In 1951, Evans resigned his seat just to prove that his constituents would endorse some proposal of his. The JLP had no prepared candidate and the Chief instructed me to run. I didn't like the idea one bit, but I allowed my name to be entered and then went off to England on other business. Miss Olga Beckford, Miss Edith Nelson, Mrs Violet Headcock and Mr Luther Morgan kept a watching brief for me, but I held no meeting, organised no campaign and, of course, I lost. The *Gleaner* was exactly right when it reported that I was the happiest loser ever seen after an election.

F.L.B. gave up his safe seat in 1955 to run against C.C.Campbell, the incumbent in Western Westmoreland, vowing to teach Campbell a lesson for having ruled against him when he was Speaker of the House. He did defeat Campbell, who was later made a Senator by Bustamante and who, after Independence in 1962, was to become the first Governor General of Jamaica. Evans eventually fell out with the PNP and after trying to form a party of his own he lost and faded from the scene.

In one of his earliest statements after the 1944 election victory, Bustamante spoke as a national leader seeing to unify his people. He said, "No section of this country or any individual who has opposed me, should have any fear that I would even attempt to do anything to hurt them. Whatever has been, whatever may still be the political differences, I shall always seek to cooperate with them in the interest of the country and the public good." But it seemed that conciliation would be an elusive thing. It was not so much the debates in the House as the arguments in the streets.

During the first term in office, the JLP was subject to harsh criticism from the small but extremely well-organised parliamentary Opposition. The PNP members were led by Florizel Glasspole, the trade unionist, and Dr Ivan Lloyd who had been in Parliament since 1942 when he won the Legislative Council seat for St Ann. Norman Manley, the PNP leader, had contested the seat in his home district, Eastern St Andrew, but he ran against three opponents: Gerald Mair of the JDP, Mary Morris Knibb, who had earlier won election to the KSAC Council as a representative of the Women's Liberal Club, and the JLP candidate, a relative unknown dermatologist, Edward Fagan, Despite being a well-known and brilliant lawyer with an impressive record in the law courts, in union and political work, Manley was defeated by Fagan. But this did not dampen the enthusiasm of his faithful few who had managed to win seats.

At this point, an event of worldwide importance must be remembered: the end of World War II. The war in Europe ended in May 1955 and, in the Far East, in August when the first atomic bomb was dropped on Hiroshima. These distant events had important effects on Jamaica. The State of Emergency came to an end; the internment camp where Bustamante had been detained for so many months was closed down; and the limitations on holding public meetings were revoked. Inevitably, the political life of the country was affected. The political climate also changed in Britain when, in the first General Elections after the war, the British people completely rejected Winston Churchill who had led the nation to victory and elected a Labour government, led by Clement Attlee. Although Bustamante had corresponded with Attlee in 1938 when he was demanding a Commission of Enquiry, the British Labour Party would be more likely to be sympathetic towards the leftist policies of the PNP than with the Jamaica Labour Party's aims of self-improvement and individual enterprise. However, trade unionism could bring the two Labour parties closer together.

Although the JLP had a big majority in the House, the Constitution did not allow the Party to act decisively on major matters. The British Governor still presided over the Executive Council on which sat five members of the House of Representatives and four from the Legislative Council. The JLP representatives, led by Bustamante as Chief Minister, could plan and propose as a team, but without the agreement of the Governor and his nominees, achievements were limited.

The Opposition made good use of those limitations and pressed the JLP hard for not doing things which they must have known could not be done. This was a legitimate strategy in the world of politics, but it did us no good. In addition, the Party had more than its fair share of bickering, particularly from those who could not endure the unaccustomed restraints of party politics. By halfway through the first term, a significant number had resigned from the Party, some to join the PNP, some to sit as Independents and others to fade into political oblivion.

The troubles of the JLP were not only internal. In mid-February, 1946, opposing forces, spearheaded by a constantly harassing TUC, called a strike at Bellevue, the Mental Hospital, in defiance of the

Government. Insane people were let loose on the streets and Bustamante himself was hit by a stone when he went to visit the institution. Having no power to direct police action, he telegraphed the Governor: *You are to take an iron hand in this matter . . . This is not a strike it is vandalism.*

Bustamante and Frank Pixley, Minister of Social Service, then went down to the waterfront and with a group of Union members marched to the Mental Hospital to help ensure a clear passage for the Sisters of Mercy who had brought food for the inmates but had been turned back when they tried to enter the institution. Unfortunately, things got out of hand at the hospital gate. One of the waterfront workers was shot and killed, and the crowd retaliated by flogging the man who had fired the gun and accusing him of threatening to shoot Busta.

The trouble escalated when the TUC leadership called other strikes involving prison warders, firemen and railway workers. The military had to take over the prisons and a fire broke out at Bellevue, resulting in the deaths of some fourteen inmates. The Government declared a State of Emergency and it was not until March that order was fully restored. In April, Bustamante and Pixley were held responsible for the deaths outside Belleview and both were charged with manslaughter. The hearing held by Chief Justice, Sir Hector Hearne, took place in Port Maria and a sensational trial resulted in an acquittal. The accused were defended by two brilliant attorneys, a Trinidadian, Sir Lennox O'Reilly, and Mr N.N.Ashenheim, a son of Lewis Ashenheim who had defended Marcus Garvey back in the thirties.

The settling of the strikes and the court case gave the Government no respite from the agitation of the PNP in the House and the TUC on the streets. At every turn, there was an argument or a dispute led by men determined to build their own cause by seeking to discredit Bustamante, the BITU and the JLP. Burdened with the growing cares of political office as well as the work of the Union, we had neither the time nor the resources to match the efforts of all those whose primary purpose was to displace Bustamante. This rivalry often became violent and always it drove divisions further into the Jamaican class structure.

A major problem on the Jamaican political scene has been caused by people seeking to get into office by exciting the expectations of the electorate far beyond what the country's means can supply. This began very early after the introduction of Adult Suffrage and during the JLP's first ten years in office. The elected government did not have the experience, the power nor the resources to solve all the problems. Yet the people were encouraged by false promises to deluge that government with demands it could not meet.

At one point, Bustamante was obliged to declare:

> There is a concentrated political plot to agitate some sections of Central Government and Local Government employees to make excessive demands for increased pay and fringe benefits and to threaten strikes. If Government were to submit to these threats it would be compelled to increase taxes in the Corporate Area and in the parishes to the extent where taxpayers, who are already hard hit, would not be able to meet the increases. This agitation and these demands are calculated to embarrass the Government. The agitators do not care whether the farmers suffer,or the unemployed eat, as long as their plot succeeds . . .
>
> The farmers must get water and roads, unemployment must be reduced, the hungry women and children must be fed, there must be money for education, the building of schools, teachers' cottages, the building of new hospitals and improvement to existing ones, and other amenities in the interest of the country. Where do these agitators expect the money to come from to meet these excessive demands? They just cannot and will not be met. Wherever there are reasonable demands, presented in a reasonable manner, consideration will be given, as has been the established practice of this Government.
>
> Our duty as Government is to protect the interests of every section of the country, not just a few agitators.

By the time the general elections of 1949 were held, we had lost a good deal of ground and the number of JLP seats was much reduced. Bustamante, who had wanted to represent a large rural constituency instead of a small one in the city, won a seat in Clarendon's sugar belt. Norman won in East St Andrew and, overall, the PNP got 13 seats to the JLP's 17 and 2 went to Independents. The calibre of the new members served to increase the standards of debate and the conduct of public business but the opposition tended to take more aggressive action on the labour and political fronts. Gradually the old class prejudices came to the fore and the idea of a united country seemed to slip away as urban voters thought little of rural voters, white-collar workers and blue-collar workers couldn't see eye to eye and uptown and downtown citizens drew lines between themselves.

This warring was not to Bustamante's liking. Despite his forthright approach to most matters, he always advocated peaceful negotiations. Although he was quick to anger he was also exceedingly quick to forgive. But at this point he began to express serious disgust with the growing conflicts and quarrelling among Jamaicans because of political differences. This was one reason why he had wanted to represent a more peaceful rural constituency and now he wanted a quiet country retreat where he could relax with friends and associates.

Isaac Barrant knew of the Chief's wishes, and one day he came into the office to report that a property in his constituency, Eastern St Thomas, was up for sale at a good price. He recommended it highly and within a few days we were making a detailed investigation that would lead to the purchasing of the near five hundred acres of Retreat Estate. It had a few acres in bananas and coconuts and extensive pastures for cattle. On it was a modest three-bedroom house, with a verandah running along three sides. Some time before, it had been used as a guest house. There were also outbuildings for staff, a pump which supplied all the water we needed and a mile of beach that was often used by people in the district and visitors from Kingston.

It was here at Retreat that we met young Seragh Lakasingh who was from Duhaney Pen. He would come to the beach on holidays and the Chief became very fond of him. Often he would sit Seragh on his knee, rock him and tell him stories. The relationship grew as the years went by and Seragh is now, as they say, 'like family'.

In our travels around the island we used to visit a BITU branch near Highgate and we would stop by a home where lived a little girl named Effie Curtis. She attended Marymount School and after graduating she became a nurse and worked at Port Antonio. She too became very close to us and is now the beloved wife of Seragh. These two have been by my side through thick and thin and remain near to my heart to this day.

Retreat soon became a centre for unofficial meetings and social engagements. We found its atmosphere greatly relaxing and Bustamante enjoyed nothing better than the hours he spent tending the animals and actually planting and reaping crops. But it was not always a joy to be there. In 1951, just two years after we had acquired the property, Jamaica was struck by the devastating Hurricane Charlie. We had gone to St Thomas to pay the workers and instead were caught in the midst of a terrible storm that wasted the plantation and severely damaged the buildings. Fortunately, no one was injured, but we were stranded for a couple of days before making it back to Kingston by way of Portland, because of the uncertain state of the shaky old Olivier Bridge which was later replaced by a new one and renamed the Bustamante Bridge. After the storm, there was a lot of work to be done in repairing the buildings and we practically rebuilt the house itself.

Some time after the hurricane, when people were expressing a need for land, we decided to cut off sections of the property for sale to small people around the Johnstown district. We disposed of a number of lots, ranging in size from two to ten acres. Afterwards, we sold some acres on the north side of the main road. Later, the house and some acres on the south, as well as the beach, were sold. Finally, when we realised that Retreat was no longer convenient for us since it was a bit too far out of Kingston, the rest of the property was bought by the Eddie Lai Corporation and we donated the water supply system to the St Thomas Parish Council.

St Thomas was truly a retreat for us. But Kingston was real life, with a government to run and a Union to expand. Jamaica made great advances during Bustamante's first two terms and greater political freedom had come with a new Constitution in 1953. However, in the third general election in 1955, the PNP finally won the power it had sought since 1938. Led by Norman Manley, the PNP took 18 seats to the JLP's 14 and so became the Government of Jamaica.

The Chief was temporarily dismayed by the defeat. However, he recovered his confidence and telegraphed the victorious Manley: *You have won a close race and now have the opportunity you have longed for. I have always taken defeat without bitterness, and triumph without boasting. We shall be an honest Opposition. Good luck.*

The JLP policies in the ten years, 1945 to 1955, still under a colonial constitution but starting on the road which would lead to independence for Jamaica, resulted in real advances. Massive drainage programmes were implemented for the Corporate Area and rural townships and also for the asphalting of rural roadways. There was industrial development: the cement factory was established; the bauxite industry had its beginnings then; the Industrial Development Corporation was set up and so was the Agricultural Development Corporation; the first industrial estate was opened at Tinson Pen. A huge primary school building programme resulted in forty primary schools being built or refurbished in a single year. The first ever government low-income housing project was built at Marverley. The airports at Kingston and Montego Bay were upgraded to bring Jamaica into the international passenger transportation age and the North Coast became the focus of tourist development. The country witnessed the promotion of women to representative positions in government and to ministerial status for the first time. The Police Force was reorganised so that Jamaicans could climb to the highest levels of authority. The University College of the West Indies was established and the University College Hospital became the teaching hospital of the West Indies. The enormous value of this institution was demonstrated in July 1954 when there was a serious outbreak of poliomyelitis that disrupted every phase of development. The authorities were able to bring the epidemic under control within less six months, although there were some cases in the following years, but of the 759 cases reported, 94 per cent were fatal. At this point, I cannot but recall the yeoman work of the late Professor John Golding who devoted so much time and skill to the treatment and rehabilitation of polio victims in Jamaica. He, together with the late Sammy Henriques and his daughter Norma, should be remembered always for the deep love and abiding interest with which they served their fellow Jamaicans.

The achievements of these years were impressive, especially considering the material resources that were available, the limited authority of the elected members and the tremendous demands that were made upon them. This was also a learning period for first-time legislators, when many of the elected members were new to the skills demanded in the development of good parliamentarians and good government.

There were those, even abroad, who noticed that Jamaica had moved ahead satisfactorily during Busta's first two terms in office. When he was voted out, the *Times* of London said of Bustamante: 'He cooperated loyally with successive Governors and under his long leadership Jamaica has seen great economic development, a marked betterment of working conditions and steadily consolidated political advances.' Alexander Bustamante's services were also recognised by Her Majesty Queen Elizabeth II who, in June 1955, bestowed on him the honour of Knight Bachelor.

11

Travelling Days

THE TEMPORARY CHANGE IN BUSTAMANTE'S ROLE IN JAMAICA as a result of the 1955 elections, provides a good opportunity to look at some of the travels I undertook with him outside Jamaica. I had driven him all over the island during the years of Union work and political campaigning,.and so I automatically accompanied him when he had to go overseas. The Chief had been a great traveller long before I went to work with him in 1936. As early as 1905, when he was twenty-one, he left Jamaica for Cuba and between then and his permanent return to the island in 1935 he had spent time not only in Cuba but also in Panama, Spain, Morocco and the United States, with visits to Jamaica in between. My longest journey had been from Montego Bay to Kingston, and little did I know how much travelling there was ahead of me. Many of the Chief's trips abroad were in the interest of Jamaican produce, mainly sugar, bananas and coffee – our traditional exports.

The first time I left Jamaica was in 1939 when I accompanied the Chief to a Trade Union Conference in Cuba. We flew there, and it was quite an adventure in those days because only seaplanes came to Jamaica. The Kingston Airport from which we departed was just a few chains from the present Cement Company and the planes had to taxi some distance across the harbour before gradually rising into the air. And, of course, we landed on the sea when we reached Havana and had to taxi to the airport on shore.

In Havana we met trade unionists from many countries. Among them was Kathleen Lewis, daughter of the great John L. Lewis who led the United Mine Workers Union in the United States from 1920 until 1960.

I can remember visiting the precinct to which the Chief had been attached when he served in the Cuban Police Force. There was only one officer still there who had served with him but this man readily recognised Bustamante and they were both glad to see each other.

Ten years after the first visit, we made another trip to Cuba, this time accompanied by the then Consul for Cuba, Dr Heriberto Clews, Mr Frank Pixley, Mr Newland and Mr Shearer. This was during the presidency of Carlos Prio Socarras who was eventually overthrown by Fulgencio Batista in 1959.

Prio invited us to the presidential palace and we were able to meet with investors who had an interest in opening a textile mill in Jamaica. This, in fact, materialised when the Ariguanabo Textile Mill was started in St Catherine.

World War II put a stop to most travel between 1939 and 1945, and so it was not until 1948 that I went on my first trip to England. We left Port Antonio in June on a banana boat, the SS Tilapia of the Elders and Fyffe Line. This vessel carried only eleven passengers and we were at sea for two weeks before getting to Liverpool where we were met by a representative of the Colonial Office and a Jamaican student, Gladstone Mills.

By a strange coincidence, a young seaman on board the Tilapia came and spoke with us, mentioning that he had seen Jamaica for the first time and how lovely he thought it was. When he gave us his name, we had a good laugh because he was Alexander Clarke, the very same as Bustamante's given name at birth. The young man invited us to his home at Cheltenham Spa and we took up the offer to see this beautiful English town. I still have an album of pictures of Cheltenham Spa and a note from him expressing his appreciation for having met me and "Mr Bustamante, such a great gentleman".

The papers in England reported that Mr Bustamante from Jamaica was in London to have an audience with His Majesty King George VI at Buckingham Palace. We also attended a Royal Garden Party at the Palace where we met for the first time Her Royal

Highness, Princess Elizabeth, later to become our present Queen. That was indeed a great experience for the country girl from Parson Reid in Westmoreland. I saw most of the places of which I had only read and pictured in my mind – the huge buildings in London, buses and trains running in every direction, Big Ben, the famous clock, and the Houses of Parliament. I enjoyed shopping at Harrods, the most famous store in the world, and eating at Martinez, run by Spaniards with whom Bustamante was very much at home, conversing in Spanish and having a really enjoyable time.

Mr Bustamante had taken his Buick motor car, A3909, with him and this created quite a stir in London as very few, if any, large cars were in evidence. The ravages of the war were still there and I was shocked to witness such destruction. We travelled around and viewed the bomb sites, visiting the poor section of London, the East End, which had been most heavily hit. Four years later, we drove there again and the Chief distributed bananas to the children there as a gesture of gratitude for the tremendous support given to Jamaica by the British after Hurricane Charlie in 1951. The English Press made the most of that occasion. However, on the 1948 visit, we made friends with many whom we met at Richmond, Kingston, Oxford, Cambridge, Windsor Castle and Liverpool. We also had discussions with Tom Driberg, Member of Parliament, at his home in Essex.

In those days there were only a few Jamaicans in London and most of them were students. Many of them had served in the war and had taken up the opportunity they had been offered to complete their education at universities there. We were happy to meet Herb McKenley and other members of Jamaica's Olympic team who were in training for the Games due to be held in London that summer. Arthur Wint and McKenley went on to win the gold and silver medals in the 400 metres.

We visited the Tower of London and saw all the historic objects there and, of course, the Crown Jewels. They were most impressive. However, there was an entertaining incident before we went into the Tower. Walking towards the entrance, Busta was quickly surrounded by a crowd of people wanting to see this unusual man of whom they had read so much. As he signed autographs and chatted with questioners, a policeman arrived and announced, "I have been sent to arrest you, sir." To this Bustamante replied, "Let's go!" The crowd was not amused and began to shout that the London Bobby wanted to take their celebrity away. The policeman led us away and then told us that he only wanted to rescue Mr B. from the crowd, otherwise he might have been there signing autographs until the next morning.

A similar incident occurred when we went to visit Windsor Castle. Again a group gathered around us and a woman shouted,"There is a King from Africa!" Someone else said, "Haven't you seen the papers? That is Bustamante from Jamaica." The Chief greeted them warmly and we went on our way to enter the Castle where we saw Queen Victoria's bedroom with all the furniture still in place.

One day we were invited to the House of Commons in order to listen to a discussion on West Indian affairs. We were entertained by some Members of Parliament and by Lord Milverton, who had been known to us as Sir Arthur Richards, Governor of Jamaica. We were meeting him for the first time since he was Governor when he had interned Bustamante under the Defence of the Realm Regulations. Lord Milverton expressed great happiness in seeing us. Busta thanked him and remarked that he would be happy to welcome and entertain him in Jamaica. In fact, Milverton did visit the island later and never failed to call on us at Tucker Avenue and at Jamaica House.

On a later visit to England, we attended a cocktail party given by Lord Milverton. On that occasion, he told Bustamante, "If I knew then what I know now, I would never have detained you." To this Busta replied, "Milord, the past has been forgotten. Your detaining me has stood me in very good stead, because, as you are aware, I am now head of the Government of Jamaica. After my release I did not fold my arms, I fought harder for the cause in which I believe." Lord Milverton said, "I am not at all surprised. You had it in you."

When Jamaica gained its Independence, Lord Milverton was one of those invited to the celebrations. He attended and we saw to it that he was well treated. He visited us at Jamaica House. As we talked, he remarked that what he admired a lot about Sir Alexander was his "wonderful gift of forgiveness". He said he had come to the realisation that his former foe was a great Jamaican, a humanitarian and a courageous fighter for justice and fair play. He felt great, he said, to know that every Christmas he and the Chief exchanged greeting cards and good wishes. To this Sir Alexander retorted, "Oh yes, Milord, but we have never exchanged jail beds."

In later years, Lord Milverton became one of the Managing Trustees of the Bustamante Foundation established in England to honour the work of Bustamante and to give scholarships to Jamaicans to study medicine, and other subjects. He served until his death and after that, his son, who was a youngster in Jamaica, became one of the Patrons. He is now an Anglican Minister – the Reverend the Right Honourable Lord Milverton.

In 1951, the Chief visited Puerto Rico as a member of the Caribbean Commission and I accompanied him. Also in the party were Mr Glegg of the Colonial Secretary's Office and Mr Theodore Sealy, editor of the Gleaner. As we arrived and were being processed by Customs, an officer came up and told Bustamante that he had instructions to see him through Immigration but that he had noticed on Busta's card that he belonged to a Communist organisation. On hearing this, Busta became very angry, as did the rest of us. He demanded to be taken to the Head of the Department as he did not intend to leave Customs until an apology was forthcoming from the United States Government.

The British Consul, who had come to meet us, offered an apology, but Bustamante insisted that the apology should come from the US Government. He remained adamant, but finally acquiesced to the pleas of the Consul who said that he was not feeling well but would see that the apology was made. And so we left. The following day a telegram with the apology was received from the US Secretary of State, Dean Rusk, who had sent it through the Governor of Puerto Rica, Munoz Marin. The incident and the response created quite a stir in Puerto Rico and after that we were treated with the greatest respect.

This and other similar humiliating and embarrassing incidents are among the events experienced on our travels. Of course, there were many pleasant and enjoyable events such as the time when a reporter interviewing Sir Alexander in New York asked, "Mr Prime Minister, I heard you were born in a thatched house built with your own hands; is that so?" The PM quickly replied, "Oh no, my son.That was your late President Lincoln; I was born in a manger!"

After my first trip to England, we returned there often, usually on government and trade business. I remember vividly a trip in 1950 when we had to fly the long route from Jamaica via the Azores and Lisbon and then take the flight to London. The deputation included Sir Robert Kirkwood, Sir Neville Ashenheim, the Hon. Rudolph Burke and the Hon. R.F. Williams. When we finally arrived in London, we had just sufficient time to drop our baggage at the hotel before hurrying to our appointment with the Secretary of State for the Colonies.

The Secretary of State was fifteen minutes late. When he finally arrived, Bustamante, the leader of the delegation, was told that the Secretary of State would be unable to give them more than fifteen minutes to state their case. Bustamante was irate. "Fifteen minutes!" he thundered, "We did not come five thousand miles to discuss very serious business in fifteen minutes. We will return home and let our people know. Come gentlemen, let us go." They all walked out.

The Secretary of State had not expected such a response, and hurriedly called back the delegation. He apologised to Sir Alexander and his party, declaring that he only meant to say fifteen minutes for that initial meeting. The Conference lasted for many days and achieved much success.

Usually when going to England, we would fly to New York to take either the Queen Mary or the Queen Elizabeth, berthing at

Southampton, then go by train to London. On our second trip via Southampton, we were invited to another Royal Garden Party at Buckingham Palace. HRH Princess Elizabeth was not yet Queen. However, we were there for her Coronation in 1953. I remember viewing the whole affair from a platform opposite Westminster Abbey where she was crowned. The Chief, as one of the official guests, was seated inside the Abbey. I sat with my old friend, Mr Westley Powell of Excelsior and Lady Allan, widow of the late sir Harold Allan. It was during this celebration that I had the honour of meeting the Queen of Tonga, who was six feet three inches tall, and the Nigerian African Chief, the Oni of Ife.

I was placed beside the Oni at one of the functions we attended, and an Englishman said to Mr Bustamante, "What a beautiful African girl that is with the One of Ife." The Chief was not amused and replied, "She is a Jamaican and she is my secretary."

During that visit, I had the pleasure of meeting some Africans from Kenya. It was during the civil war and Jomo Kenyatta, the leader of the Kikuyu, was in exile or in prison.The Kenyans told us how they had read about Bustamante and had greatly admired him. It was their wish that we would come to visit Kenya to assist them in the struggle for freedom and justice and political independence. Bustamante gave them words of encouragement and promised to visit, if at all possible. It was one of our great regrets that we were never able to pay the promised visit; and Busta constantly spoke of the struggling people of Africa.

In 1954 we were back in England and Bustamante, as Chief Minister, attended a glittering 'welcome home' luncheon put on for Queen Elizabeth by the Lord Mayor of London. The function took place in the stately Egyptian Room at the Mansion House,the official residence of the Lord Mayor. Bustamante was seated with thirty other selected guests at the high table. Soon after the luncheon started, he was seen by Sir Winston Churchill who waved a friendly recognition, at which Bustamante smiled and waved back. All heads turned to see the two statesmen greeting each other.

On the return trip, we stopped over in New York and also visited Connecticut where we were received by the Governor of the State. We visited Jamaican farm workers located there. This was our second visit. In 1953 we had toured the farm camps in Connecticut, along with the Chief Liaison Officer, Mr Herbert McDonald, (later Sir Herbert) and our Minister of Agriculture, the Hon. Isaac Barrant. On that trip we also went to New York and were received by Mayor Vincent Impellitteri and also met with attorney James Watson, son of the famous Jamaican-born judge of the same name. Mrs Watson, widow of the judge, was also present.

When we were travelling by way of New York, we often stopped there or in Washington either on official business or to visit friends. For example, in New York in 1952 the Chief took me to visit the Joint Diseases Hospital where he had worked for some years before returning to Jamaica. He found one of the physicians, Dr Galub, still working there. Dr Galub gave him a warm welcome and when this old friend enquired of him what he was doing for himself, Busta told him that he was Chief Minister of the Government of Jamaica and that he was on his way to London to discuss trade with the British Government.

Dr Galub remarked that he was not surprised at the turn of events. However, he added, the hospital had not been able to replace Busta's dedicated services. They had replaced him with a woman, but he should feel free to return for his old job if the occasion ever arose. We had a good time with the doctor but not long afterwards he passed on. After becoming Prime Minister, Bustamante also corresponded with Mrs Sidney Livingston whose husband had been manager of the Joint Diseases Hospital when Busta worked there. Also on this same trip we met Mr Wendell Malliet, the Jamaican-born editor of the Amsterdam News, the leading black newspaper of that time.

In 1957 we went on a private trip to Europe, taking in London, Rome, Paris and Barcelona. While we were in Rome, we visited the Colosseum and St Peter's Basilica. Busta also had an audience with Pope Pius XII at the Vatican and we took time out to entertain some

Jamaicans who were there studying for the priesthood. They were Peter Figueroa, Jack Roper, Stanley Shearer, Vincent Campbell and Colin Bryan. Colin, a little older than the others, had served in World War II and later at the Colonial Office in London.

We spent three days in Paris and went on to Barcelona in Spain, where Bustamante had spent some of his more youthful years. He tried, but could not find some of the old familiar places because the massive damage done by bombing during the Spanish Civil War had turned the place upside down. While we were staying at a hotel in Barcelona, we were quietly informed about a Royal refugee who was hiding there from revolutionaries. We were told how he constantly changed his dress and used disguises to conceal his identity and confound anyone searching for him. From Barcelona we flew to Palma in Majorca where we had a few restful days.

In 1963, on a sad occasion, we flew to Washington to attend the funeral of John F. Kennedy. We were accompanied by the Chief of Staff of the Jamaica Defence Force, Brigadier Paul Crook, and the Commissioner of Police, Noel Crosswell. In Washington we assembled at the White House with other special visitors, including General Charles de Gaulle and Prince Philip of England. We all walked from the White House along the route to the church, following the coffin which rested on a gun-carriage. After the service, we were taken by car to Arlington National Cemetery for the interment.

The Chief's last overseas trip on official business was in the same year, when we visited the Dominican Republic to attend the inauguration of President Juan Bosch. We were joined there by parliamentarians Robert Lightbourne, Herbert Eldemire, Roy McNeil, John Gyles and Clem Tavares. Bosch was forced out of office shortly after his installation and I remember that Bustamante had privately predicted that he would not be long in office because he had been living abroad for a long time and had just returned to the country.

After this, Busta's travelling days were more or less over, except for medical reasons, and it would not be long before he would decide to retire to the cool heights of Irish Town. We had journeyed long and far together and shared memories of great international occasions and visits with good friends. Even though I would continue my own travels after he was gone, nothing can erase my memories of those remarkable travelling days we had together.

12

From Defeat to Victory

DEFEAT IN THE 1955 GENERAL ELECTIONS, though seen as a real possibility, was a disappointment to the Chief and to those of us who felt strongly that his leadership had provided a sure foundation for the future development of the island. However, transfer of the weight of responsibility of government could have provided him with an opportunity to rest and reflect. He was already past his seventieth birthday and had been extremely active, mentally and physically, for some twenty years without a break. I was not the only one to advise him to take it easy for a while but he would not hear of it. He said he had to rebuild the Party, provide a vigorous Opposition in Parliament and continue his labours for the workers in and out of the BITU.

I myself wanted some rest from the strenuous work that had fallen to my lot at the BITU. I had been treasurer from the outset but, with time, my duties had extended to those of a sort of overseer of the organisation. Because of my practical experience and knowledge of the working of the Union, everyone would turn to me whether we were in a crisis or dealing with routine affairs. It was rewarding work but it was also exhausting.

At the same time, while the Chief was concentrating on the running of the Government, the leaders and field workers of the TUC made it their primary business to erode the position of the BITU. Instead of directing their efforts at organising employees in establishments which were still non-unionised, they repeatedly turned their attention to places where the BITU already represented the workers and then they would set about 'raiding' the BITU members, trying to add them to their own organisations. These tactics demanded a speedy response and also used up the energy that might have been spent in consolidating hard-won gains in the workplace. In spite of this, our membership grew over the years and in 1955 we were still the largest of the unions.

The rest I sought was not to be. I was not only the 'Jill of all trades' in the Union, I was private secretary to the President-General who was also the Leader of the Party and the Leader of the Opposition. The Chief had also been keeping a watchful eye on the developing of the West Indies Federation, which had been proposed in 1947. On his way to that Montego Bay Conference, he had stated his position on Federation with great clarity He said: " I am going with an open mind to visualise and fathom the minds of the experts and to subject to severe scrutiny public opinion, criticism and judgment, whether or not there is anything as good as self-government for the West Indies' political, social and economic advancement in Federation. Depend on me, I am going there with one express purpose, to see if Federation is for the good of the West Indies and, particularly, Jamaica.

"I am going to Montego Bay to find out if there is going to be a large loan programme, how and when it will be raised, how it will be distributed among the islands, through what source and what will be the ultimate financial costs to the colonies, particularly Jamaica. I must be aware of the personnel of the central ruling body who will work in unity with the Governor General, who is likely to be Governor General, what power will the central governing body hold over the economic and social destiny of the islands and how much power will be vested in them to guide and interfere with the affairs of each island. I must know how and what inter-island trading will mean and what one colony had to sell to another colony that does not produce the same product . . ."

At that time he had supported the idea in principle, declaring that he was for a viable regional government, but not "a federation of paupers, foisted by Britain to escape her . . . responsibilities." And when the British representative, Arthur Creech Jones, said to the conference, "I put it to you that it is essential to the progress of the West Indies that we should get along the road to Federation as quickly as we can," Busta remarked that he should not pitchfork it down the throats of the delegates.

Plans for the Federation did proceed rather quickly with the enthusiasm of the Eastern Caribbean territories and the Jamaican Government led by Norman Manley. Just three years after the 1955 elections in Jamaica we were faced with Federal Elections. Manley had been made President of the West Indies Federal Labour party and enjoyed good support from some of the leading personalities in the region. However, the JLP defeated the PNP and took twelve of the seventeen Federal seats allocated to Jamaica. Finally, the overall victory went to the West Indies Federal Labour Party. When the winning candidates not affiliated with the WIFLP decided to weld themselves into an organised opposition, Busta was selected to lead that party, the Democratic Labour Party. Like Mr Manley, the Chief did not seek a seat and was not a member of the Federal Parliament, but it meant still more work for Gladys Longbridge.

Down in Trinidad, Eric Williams's party, the PNM, had also been defeated in the Federal election. Since he and Manley were outside the Federal Government, the WIFLP selected Grantley Adams of Barbados to be Prime Minister of the new government. This put Bustamante into stronger opposition than before since he had little faith in Adams. Finally, when Jamaica was considering setting up an oil refinery, Adams spoke of the power of the Federal Government to impose retroactive taxation on affiliated territories, Busta felt that the time had come for a showdown. He had already stated that he wished that the Federation would be smashed to nothing if it meant having a Customs Union that would throw Jamaicans out of work. The talk of retroactive taxation was, therefore, the last straw.

The Federation was not six months old and already there was talk of Jamaica's secession. The JLP was determined to make it an issue in the general elections due the following year. The contest was fought in July 1959 and the margin of the PNP's victory by number of seats was increased astonishingly, although the percentage difference in votes was roughly 10 per cent, the same as in 1955. No doubt this had something to do with the increased number of seats, from 32 to 45, and the reshaping of constituency boundaries.

In the wake of this second defeat, some observers felt that the time had come for the JLP to become more organised and less dependent on the personal popularity of its leader. The *Daily Gleaner*, for examplee, described our team as akin to an 'unmarshalled collection of individuals'. But that was not quite true. The process of reorganisation had already begun with such outstanding politicians as Donald Sangster, Clement Tavares, Robert Lightbourne, Herbert Eldemire and Rose Leon. Young Edward Seaga had also come into the party at Busta's invitation and was making a most useful contribution. The Chief nominated him to the Legislative Council and, at twenty-nine, he was the youngest member ever to sit in that Council. Later he became a Senator and, finally, in 1962, Busta persuaded him to run in West Kingston, as he thought that Seaga's close practical experience with people at the grassroots would make him the right choice for that constituency. He has held that constituency for thirty-five years.

Edward Seaga has been a tremendous asset to the Party. He has been a tower of strength to us and his loyalty unswerving. Over the years, his contribution to the development of Jamaica is worthy of the highest praise and commendation. Not once has he failed to rally to the aid of this country, even under the most trying and exacting circumstances. His care and concern for me at all times have created a close bond between us and I remember how proud I felt on November 1, 1980, when I attended his Swearing-in as Jamaica's fifth Prime Minister. Today he holds the record as the longest- serving Member of Parliament in our country, an achievement worthy of the greatest recognition.

The Federal controversy continued. Robert Lightbourne had resigned from the Federation and now sat in the Jamaican House of Representatives. Edwin Allen, who had lost his seat in Clarendon in 1959, was being considered to run for the vacant Federal seat, but by

His Imperial Majesty
Haile Selassie
also visited Jamaica in 1966

Sir Alex and Lady B.welcome President and Mrs Kenneth Kaunda of Zambia. Deputy Prime Minister, the Hon. Donald Sangster (far right) and the Minister of Foreign Affairs, the Hon. Hector Wynter, look on.

His Highness, Prince Philip, Duke of Edinburgh, made a second visit that year to open the Commonwealth Games. He was accompanied by Prince Charles and Princess Anne, seen here in lively conversation.

A Reception Room

The Swimming Pool

The Central Patio

The Ballroom arranged for a formal banquet

The Kitchens

The Prime Minister's Office

A serious moment at Jamaica House

The Double Staircase from above

A Guest Bedroom

The Entrance to the Prime Minister's Apartments

The Double Staircase in the Entrance Hall of Jamaica House

At Jamaica House, Donald Sangster congratulating Sir Alex on his 83rd birthday

1969. Lady B. arriving at Kingston Parish Church for the funeral of Norman Manley

Prime Minister Michael Manley at Bellencita, offering condolences to Lady B. on the death of Sir Alexander, August 1977.

Members of the Manley family and friend gather round Lady B. on the death if Sir Alexander..

Governor General Sir Florizel Glasspole presents Lady B. with the commemorative postal stamps issued in honour of Sir Alexander

Lady B., on a happier occasion, with friends and family at Bellencita. Far left: Effie Lakasingh.

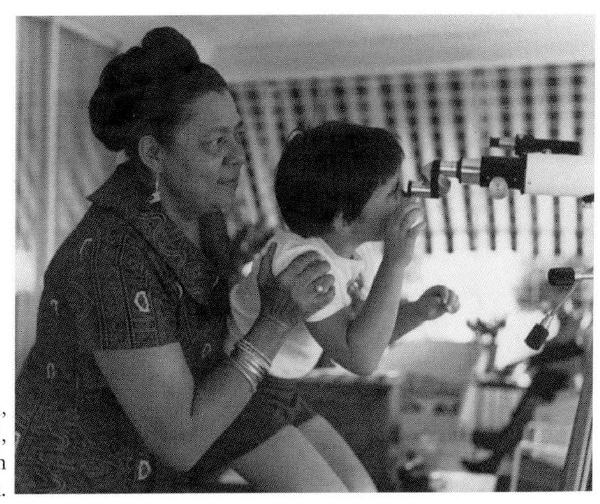

Lady B. helps her godson, Anoop Dadlani, to view the city through her telescope at Bellencita.

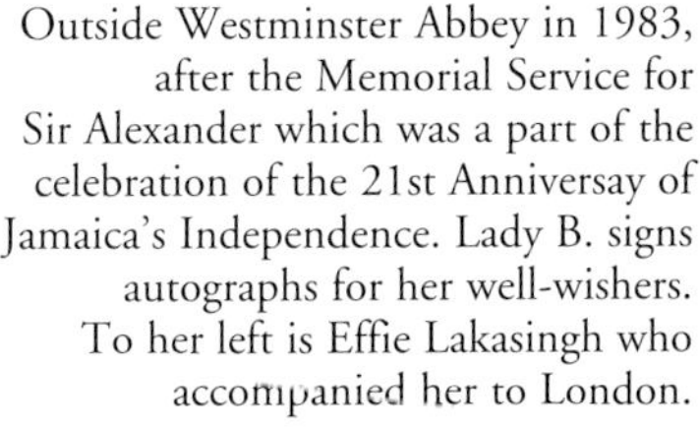

Outside Westminster Abbey in 1983, after the Memorial Service for Sir Alexander which was a part of the celebration of the 21st Anniversay of Jamaica's Independence. Lady B. signs autographs for her well-wishers. To her left is Effie Lakasingh who accompanied her to London.

The Captain cuts the cake for Lady B.'s 77th birthday on board the S/S *Celebration* during a Caribbean cruise . From left: Mrs Shirley Braham; Alvin Thompson; Seragh Lakasingh; Joyce Chen Sue; Donald Braham.

Lady B, at home, playing her Hammond organ

Lady B. at home with friends

With John Issa and his wife, Aida, with their daughters, Zein and Muna

Lady B. happily at home at Bellencita in 1997

1951 Buick

LADY B. & HER CARS

Lady B. has always loved to drive
the finest top-of-the-line cars.
She drove Bustamante all over Jamaica
during the Trade Union and early political days.
As a result, she knows the island
from end to end in detail and can find
even the remotest country districts.

Miss G, at the wheel of her new aqua and white Plymouth in 1956

Miss Gladys Longbridge with her Buick

Lady B. and her 1960 Galaxy

The pale blue Cadillac at Bellencita

The silver-grey Lincoln Versailles 1980

The new custom-built Rover 800 Series 1997

The Lincoln Town Car 1991

1960 a decision had been taken not to contest the seat and, in addition, to oppose Jamaica's continued involvement with the Federation. Norman Manley reacted at once. Six months earlier, he had rejected a proposal made by D.C. Tavares that a referendum be held to determine whether the people of Jamaica wanted to continue in the Federation or not. Now he changed his mind and announced that there would be a referendum to settle the question once and for all.

Having won the 1959 elections, the PNP must have been confident that the JLP would again be defeated, but no date for the referendum wasset. The issue dragged on for a year during which the JLP conducted a vigorous anti-Federation campaign while Manley kept trying to salvage the image of the regional government. In mid-1961, the Jamaica Labour Party surprised the government when L.G.Newland submitted an amendment during a House debate that the Government of Jamaica request the British Government " . . . to take the necessary steps to introduce legislation to grant Jamaica Independence on the 23rd May 1962 . . ." In so doing, he formalised the JLP's position and, at the same time, put on the legislative record the island's first official call for independence. Manley, backed into a position where he was obliged to reject the amendment, went down in Hansard as voting against the very self-government that he had advocated for more than two decades.

The date for the Referendum was set for 19 September 1961. During the campaign, Manley tried to reassure the voters that he would go and head the Federal Government to protect Jamaica's interests. While the JLP insisted that Jamaica was able and entitled to govern its own affairs, the PNP's theme was that Jamaica could not go it alone. In the end, 54 per cent of the voters said no to Federation. Jamaica had taken the first step to nationhood and it was Bustamante and the JLP that could rightly claim the credit.

In the following months, Jamaican leaders showed rare unanimity in working out the preliminaries for Independence. Manley, although out-manoeuvered, was in fact a true advocate of Independence, and

Bustamante, always chivalrous in triumph was forever respectful of his cousin's innate integrity. The two had no difficulty in arriving at an Independence Constitution which was thought to be appropriate for the times and the conditions. It was Manley who led the discussions in London and he justified the non-radical form of the Constitution by saying: "We had a system which we understood; we had been operating it for many years with sense. It is a system that has endured in other countries for generations successfully. It is a system that is consistent with the sort of ideals we have in this country, and it was not difficult to decide that we should follow that familiar system with those modifications which we thought the circumstances of independence deserved."

In the General Elections of April 1962, the Jamaican electorate returned Bustamante and the Jamaica Labour Party to power once more. The JLP gained 50.4 per cent of the popular vote while the PNP had 48.59 per cent. Bustamante and his team now had the awesome responsibility of leading the Jamaican people into and during their first years of political Independence. Self-government, for which Busta had said we were not ready in 1944, was now ours and it was his task, at the age of seventy-eight, to make it work. He had never made any apology for the patient preparation which the process involved. Once he had remarked to a group of impatient workers, " . . . you must learn to creep before you climb," and on another occasion, in the House of Representatives, he said, "Mr Speaker, the Lord set an example for us. He could have taken one minute or even one second to build this world, but he did it in six days . . . He was setting an example for us sinners, and I prefer to follow the Lord's example by going a little slow." And he added, "It takes three weeks for a hen to hatch an egg. The Lord could have made it possible for the hen to hatch that egg overnight."

We could certainly have used a little more time than we had in the preparations for Independence. So much had to be done in those few months. Gordon House, the new seat of Parliament, had still to be completed and the National Stadium as well, and all the preparations made for big celebrations all across the island. Black, gold and green Jamaican flags had to be made, including little ones for all the schoolchildren, and accommodations found for the many visitors. People who were not so keen on the idea of Independence said that the Stadium could not be finished on time while some malicious people spread a completely unfounded rumour that there would be rioting after the Independence Ceremony at the Stadium and that all the machetes in Kingston had been sold out. Nothing could be further from the truth: there was dancing in the streets instead.

The story of that night has often been told elsewhere. My lasting memories are of the final seconds of August 5 and the total darkness of the National Stadium and the silence of all the people there until the first moment of August 6 when a single beam of light shone on the Jamaican flag flying officially for the first time in the place of the British red, white and blue. Everyone in the Stadium cheered. I remember the big fireworks show, with the flag displayed in fireworks: the Chief, very much Sir Alexander Bustamante, dancing with Princess Margaret at the Independence Ball at the new Sheraton Hotel in New Kingston (now the Wyndham Hotel, but it did not have a tower then); and meeting Vice-President Lyndon Johnson, who was there as the personal representative of President Kennedy. I also have a more personal memory. At some point in the celebrations at the National Stadium, the bracelet I was wearing dropped off my hand but I did not notice it at the time, partly because I was wearing long white gloves for such a formal occasion. Somehow a little report appeared in the Gleaner about my loss and on the next day the precious bracelet which I valued greatly was returned to me by the police officer who had found it and dropped it into his pocket. I have that bracelet to this day.

It seemed as if the patience that the Chief had so often shown in public matters extended to his private life and also to me. I had admired, respected and loved Bustamante from my earliest association with him. Our relationship, built on mutual confidence and shared hopes for our country, was as strong as any could be. Yet the question of marital status had not been much discussed, because he did not believe in divorce and in 1933 he had made such a commitment to Sophie Townsend, a Canadian nurse, who was still alive when he returned to Jamaica. He had repeatedly invited her to live with him in Jamaica, but she would have preferred him to return to the United States. Over the years, their correspondence grew less and less and they drifted apart. She passed away in 1958, leaving much of what she owned to Bustamante but he would not accept the bequest and asked for it to be turned over to her relatives.

Many have asked how and when Bustamante proposed to me. The short answer is, he did not. He just announced to me one day that he was going to marry me in a Roman Catholic ceremony and that I should begin to prepare for the event. He had been so busy with the cares of office that I had never imagined that he had marriage on his mind. No doubt he knew very well what my answer would be, so I passed over the usual niceties and spared the gallant gentleman the formality of going down on bended knee. Since I had to become a Roman Catholic, I was given instruction in this religion by Father Stanley Shearer at the North Street Cathedral.

The wedding, conducted by Father Stanley Shearer and Father Gladstone Wilson, took place at 21 Hopefield Avenue, now the residence of the Roman Catholic Bishop of Jamaica, the Most Reverend Edgerton Clarke, on September 7, 1962. My maid-of-honour was a close friend and neighbour, Vie Wattley, and Hugh Shearer was the best man. The entire Cabinet attended and Donald Sangster, who came to 'give me away', jovially remarked, "How am I going to give away what I want for myself?" Busta chuckled and replied, "Son, too bad for you." To make a long and beautiful story short, we took the vows, pledged eternal loyalty to each other, and went off to England for a honeymoon that same day and, in true storybook fashion, returned to our great homeland to live together happily ever after.

However, we did take a side trip to New York on the way home so that Sir Alexander could raise the flag of Jamaica at the United Nations Building on September 18. That too was a memorable ceremony. We met the first Secretary-General of the United Nations, U Thant of Burma, for the first time. Sir Alexander invited him to make a visit to Jamaica and this he did before long.

Back in Jamaica, Bustamante threw himself fully into the task of building this newly independent nation. The reorganized, rejuvenated Jamaica Labour Party was well equipped to shape the destiny of the country. Enthusiasm among parliamentarians was unmatched and their talent was of a high standard.

For the first two years of Independence, the Chief carried the same zeal and determination that he always had into his work, always projecting the thought that nothing but the best was good enough. He was a source of inspiration to his Ministers and indeed to all Members of Parliament. Sometimes he seemed to defy the laws of nature to accomplish a task once he had undertaken it on behalf of the country.

One project that interested him was the building of Jamaica House. He felt strongly that the Prime Minister of the country should have a suitable residence and that it should be built on the grounds of King's House, for many years the home of the British Governors. It had been suggested to the Chief that, as the Prime Minister, he should live at Vale Royal, the house that had been occupied by the Colonial Secretary, but he refused, pointing out that our house on Tucker Avenue was more commodious and better suited for entertaining guests. Construction of Jamaica House, designed by Lloyd Shearer and Morrison, was begun in 1963, and the contractor, Vasco Coombs, did a fine job. Meanwhile we stayed on at Tucker Avenue until the day in 1964 when we moved into the impressive house built as the residence for the then and future Prime Ministers of Jamaica. It was built around a courtyard with the public rooms at the front for formal occasions, including a ballroom, and guest bedrooms on the floor above. Across the courtyard were the rooms designed as the private quarters of the

Prime Minister. There was a swimming pool on the north side, but that has now been built over for more office accommodation. I too had a hand in the development of the site since I was involved in the design of the flower beds on either side of the long drive leading up to the front drive.

The Chief and I lived and worked there until 1967, when he retired from public life. We entertained many important visitors, some of them internationally famous, in a manner suitably befitting an independent country. I am sorry to see that this once dignified symbol of our nationhood has now become offices rather than a home for the head of Jamaica's government. The pride that people had in pointing to Jamaica House and saying, "That is where our Prime Minister lives," has been taken away. It is my hope that one day the people of Jamaica will be sufficiently concerned to ensure that Jamaica House serves the purpose for which it was built and paid for out of public funds.

On February 24, 1964, Bustamante celebrated his eightieth birthday at the Sheraton (now the Wyndham) Hotel, but his health was fading and he began the gradual process of handing over authority to his Deputy Prime Minister, Donald Sangster. The Chief's vision was deteriorating, and in that same year he travelled to Washington, DC, for treatment at the Walter Reed Military Hospital. Fully ten years before, Dr Evelyn had advised him to do something about his eyes, but he would always put his work before his health. Surgery was carried out on his left eye, but no sooner had he returned from Washington than he plunged straight into work again.

Bustamante steadily ignored the advice and concern of everyone, doctors, friends, admirers and myself alike, when we told him to take time for a little rest. As a result, his health slipped further down. Finally, after the 1967 General Elections, he officially retired from active public life and moved out of Jamaica House. It was then that we retired to our own new home which we had built on the road to Irish Town. Before Sir Alex moved out of Jamaica House, the Queen bestowed on him the Knight Grand Cross of the Order of the British Empire (GBE). The award was announced to the country on the Queen's Birthday that year. Since British honours are no longer accepted in our country, Sir Alex may well go down in history as the only Jamaican Prime Minister to be distinguished by such an honour.

In my view, Jamaica has never had a better balanced team of legislators and the fruits of their work during the first ten years of Independence are there today to support my claim. The machinery for progressive government was soundly constructed, the economy had grown significantly and the social services were greatly improved. Urban development was moving well and the transformation from colonial to independent government was visible both here and abroad. Jamaica made impressive advances in a relatively short space of time. But it was not enough to satisfy those, especially in the PNP, who said that they could do better. They were constantly criticising and in a manner calculated to cause bitter disaffection and divisions within the society.

What happened in Jamaica after those first ten years of progress as a young independent nation is well documented elsewhere and there is no need for me to recount any of it in these pages. However, the record must show why in that period I found it necessary to refuse to accept the honour of Order of Jamaica for the services I had rendered to my country. It was in 1979 that the offer was made to me and it was to be announced officially on the day that Sir Alexander's shrine was to be dedicated at National Heroes Park. I was on my way to the ceremony that day when someone stopped my car and advised me not to attend as political hooligans had overrun the place and were firing guns indiscriminately. People were running for cover and it was absolutely unsafe to go anywhere near the scene. I turned back and when the report was later confirmed, I advised the government that in no way would I accept the award until decency prevailed and proper respect was accorded to my late husband. This finally happened in 1983 and I was pleased to be honoured in circumstances appropriate to a civilised community.

The spite and bitterness of the 1970s, the intensive efforts made to divide the people and discredit the contribution of others who had gone before, had never before been so much in evidence, not even during the worst days of imperial rule. The vile campaign against Bustamante, a National Hero, had been started long before the disgraceful demonstration at Heroes Park, and those in authority had done little to stem the tide of ingratitude and dissension. For instance, in April of 1978, eleven years after Bustamante's retirement from public life and less than a year after his death, five PNP members of the Portland Parish Council supported a motion seeking to besmirch his name and to remove his portrait from the walls of the Council chamber.

I have no pleasure in recounting the incident, but the people of Jamaica should be reminded of what the country endured at that time and what we must be careful to avoid in the future. The motion moved by Councillor Larry Robertson and seconded by Councillor Charles Rhoden paid scant respect or appreciation for the known sacrifices made by Bustamante and instead read:

> Whereas scientific research and analysis has shown that William Alexander Bustamante has divided the working class movement in Jamaica during the period (September 1942) setting back our people's struggle, And whereas Bustamante is to be blamed for most of our problems, including crime, violence and unemployment, Be it resolved that this Council vote in condemnation of Bustamante and remove his photograph from the Council's chamber and also to ask that the Government remove the National Hero status from this bandit.

What ingratitude to a person who had suffered so much!

During the debate that followed, the detractors were so vicious in their remarks that the Mayor had to urge them to exercise restraint in their choice of language. Fortunately, although the JLP did not have a single member in the Council, there were six other PNP Councillors who were more considerate and more mindful of truth and history.

They were led by Councillor L.A.Fairweather of Fairy Hill and included Councillors Gloria Bailey, H.E.Davis of Rio Grande Valley, Bailey, Cousins, Smith and McCarthy. Seven others, who seem to have had no guts, declined to vote.

In countering the denigrators, Councillor Fairweather said:

> As far as I am aware, only one Adam was created. As such, I regard the man Bustamante as my brother. If at this late stage we wait until the man is dead and in his grave . . . to flog him, I cannot be a party to that. To be perfectly fair to the dead man and his widow, we must realise that when the PNP, our party, in two recent elections won all eighteen seats to the Portland Parish Council and two seats to parliament, some of the people who voted us that victory must have been supporters of the JLP. And in fairness to those and all the people of Portland and to Bustamante's widow, I cannot go along with such a resolution.

Responding to Rhoden's uncomplimentary remarks about Bustamante's wealth as compared with Norman Manley's comparative lack of financial resources, Councillor Fairweather said:

> I suspect that if Bustamante had died a pauper, his portrait would have been allowed to remain on the walls of the roads and on those of the Council's chamber. If in Bustamante's lifetime he made a fortune that was his good luck. Removing now his portrait from the Council's walls will not get machetes for the farmers and help poor mothers get soap to wash their children's clothes. In that view, I move a counter motion that his portrait shall remain on the walls of the Council's chamber.

Councillor Davis recalled how Bustamante, when he was leader of the country, had given 'special and sympathetic treatment' to a PNP delegation of which he was a member. He refused to support the resolution for condemnation and helped to defeat the plan by six votes to five with five abstentions. Thus did they preserve the integrity of the Portland Parish Council and the people they represented.

What needs to be remembered about the JLP's two terms of office in the first decade of Jamaica's Independence is the astonishing progress made between 1962 and 1972. Nothing since that time has come anywhere near to those accomplishments and little credit has been given to the JLP for what was achieved then. During those years, fifty-nine Junior Secondary Schools and over forty Primary Schools were built. The Teachers' Colleges were improved and expanded and all the tertiary educational institutions were upgraded. Technical education was made free of cost to all students and the Student Loan Fund was established to aid students at the University of the West Indies, the College of Arts and Technology and the Teachers' Colleges.

In 1972 the country was told that the JLP did not pay sufficient attention to social welfare, yet in the ten years before that we had launched an unprecedented 100-village programme and carried out development programmes in them to upgrade local communities. The campaign for literacy and adult education had been expanded and thousands of young people had been trained in the arts, crafts and trades. A programme called the National Volunteers Organisation to provide skills training for young people was also set up and those involved were encouraged to help the aged and the indigent. Youth training was expanded at Cobbla and Chestervale while new camps were opened at Kenilworth in Hanover, Lluidas Vale in St Catherine and Cape Clear in St Mary. National Insurance was introduced, at first strongly opposed by PNP propagandists who turned the NIS backwards and called the programme SIN!

In the field of health, the first government in Independence built the May Pen Hospital, the Savanna-la-Mar Hospital, the Cornwall Regional Hospital and the Bustamante Hospital for Children, the first of its kind in the Caribbean. In fact, after Independence, the British Army passed on their military hospital to the government of Jamaica. It was the Chief's idea to remove the children from the overcrowded Kingston Public Hospital and transform the buildings at Up Park Camp into a specialist hospital for them. I have been the patron of this hospital ever since it was declared open.

The Jamaica Cultural Development Commission was established to encourage various forms of cultural expression. Television was introduced into Jamaica; National Honours, including the Order of National Hero, were instituted and the process of identifying those to be so honoured began. The first important step in this regard was the bringing back of the remains of Marcus Garvey to be interred at National Heroes Park.

In other areas of development there was the launching of Air Jamaica and the founding of the Urban Development Corporation that rebuilt the waterfronts of Kingston, Ocho Rios and Montego Bay, and provided a modern profile for Negril. The Jamaicanisation programme came into being and embraced all interests in the country. In this regard, the country recorded its greatest financial and economic advancement in modern history and experienced and average growth rate of six per cent, among the highest levels of economic achievement worldwide.

All this progress was achieved without any crisis in management and without asking the International Monetary Fund for a cent. Economic woes came later, but the two JLP administrations in the first years of Jamaica's Independence had left a solid foundation on which to build.

13

Bellencita 1967-1997

WHILE WE WERE LIVING AT JAMAICA HOUSE, the Chief found it very relaxing to go for drives, whenever possible, in the hills of St Andrew. There was one spot we liked very much on the road to Irish Town, a piece of open land, on a plateau, with a commanding view of the city and mountains. We used to get out of the car and sit there under a mango tree, enjoying the view and the cool air. One day, the Chief asked the caretaker who was the owner of the property. He told us that it belonged to Mr Kennedy of Grace, Kennedy, and added that he knew for a fact that it was not for sale. Busta thanked him for the information, and said nothing more.

The following week, Sir Alexander summoned Hugh Shearer, and requested him to go and see the owner, Mr Luis Fred Kennedy, and tell him that Bustamante was very seriously interested in acquiring this property. Hugh immediately went to see Mr Kennedy and told him that Sir Alex would like to build his retirement home on that spot, especially as he preferred a cool, tranquil climate to the bustling city.

Mr Kennedy quickly replied, "My son, I am not selling it, you know, but I cannot tell Busta no." When Sir Alex heard the reply, he told Shearer to say to Mr Kennedy, "Just name the price." Negotiations began immediately for this seventeen-acre property, and were rapidly concluded to our mutual satisfaction.

The architectural plans for the house were soon drawn up by Lloyd Shearer, and the construction, again supervised by Vasco Coombs, got under way in 1966. The house was completed by

February 1967. General Elections were held on February 27 and we moved from Jamaica House into our new home on March 31. I have lived there ever since.

Even though we were moving to our own house, built on exactly the spot we had chosen, I felt some regret when we left Jamaica House. Bustamante was the first Jamaican Prime Minister to live there, and we seemed to have developed a close relationship with the house itself. We had many fond memories of it and many important events had taken place there. Just before leaving on his retirement, Sir Alex had been awarded the Lebanese National Honour of the Cedars of Lebanon by that Government and the Honorary Consul of Lebanon, the late George Shoucair, had come to Jamaica House to make the presentation to him.

We had entertained notable guests at Jamaica House. Her Majesty the Queen Mother, visited us there in 1965, Her Majesty Queen Elizabeth II and her husband Prince Philip came in 1966 and, later that year, Prince Philip with Prince Charles and Princess Ann arrived for the Commonwealth Games. Princess Alice of Athlone and His Imperial Majesty Haile Selassie, also visited us in Jamaica House in the same year. Then, at different times, we entertained the first British High Commissioner to Jamaica, and Lady Morley, who also visited us at Bellencita, the Hon. Kenneth Kaunda and Mrs Kaunda of Zambia, President Tubman of Liberia ambassadors of various countries, the ordinary man on the street and, funnily enough, an escapee from Bellevue Mental Hospital. We were soon to discover that, although we no longer lived in Jamaica House, old friends and new were very willing to come to see us in our new home in the hills.

It was Sir Alex who chose the name of the house, 'Bellencita'. He told me that it was Spanish for 'a nice little person', and explained that with me constantly in his mind, he could not have come up with a more appropriate name. I was very happy with it.

I can never forget the tremendous work involved and the wonderful job done by my close friends, Mrs Violet Wattley and my secretary

Mrs Monica Wells, in organising the removal and preparing the house so that it would be a comfortable home for us. I was keenly interested in the landscaping and making a garden and I will always be grateful to the late Vernon James, Superintendent of Public Gardens at the Royal Botanical Gardens at Hope, for all the assistance and advice he gave me in the laying out of the grounds. He it was who introduced the exotic plants and unusual trees. The lychee trees were introduced by Dr Aubrey McFarlane and many of them are still growing there. By 1968 Mr James had even cultivated a new bougainvillea hybrid for my garden, a brilliant, glowing red, spectacular in full bloom, and named it Lady Bustamante. It still brightens the verandah overlooking Kingston.

Bellencita was a home which generated much happiness and light-heartedness. There was a constant flow of visitors, as well as close friends and relatives, and we never felt lonely. Among our welcome visitors were Olive Lewin and the Jamaica Folk Singers who often came to share their music with us. We also welcomed a group of children from Jericho All Age School in Hanover who, headed by their Principal, had come to sing and dance for us. We had world famous visitors as well, such as the Archbishop of Canterbury, the Governor General of Canada and Mrs Michener, Alan Lennox-Boyd, retired Secretary of State for the Colonies, President Figueres of Costa Rica and other leaders of the Caribbean. Ambassadors from many countries came regularly to pay their respects as did many important visitors to Jamaica.

Although he had retired from active political life, Sir Alex always kept well abreast of what was happening, both in Government and in the BITU. He was kept well informed by government Ministers and by his earlier colleagues who came to Bellencita not only to tell him of the latest developments but also to ask for his advice. No one could match his experience and practical knowledge of Jamaican politics and trade union affairs.

There were still notable occasions. It was on 26 August 1967 that the Resident Ambassador of the Republic of China (Taiwan), His Excellency Mr Patrick Sun, visited us at Bellencita to present to Sir

Alexander the Distinguished Order of the Brilliant Star with Special Cordon from his Government in recognition of Sir Alexander's excellent relationship with the Chinese, especially those in Jamaica. Two years later, the Venezuelan Government presented Sir Alex with the decoration of the Order of the Liberator in the Class of Grand Cordon, in recognition of his outstanding achievement as a world figure. Among the other honours he received during these years, he especially valued the degree of Doctor of Laws, which he received *Honoris Causa* from the University of the West Indies. Princess Alice of Athlone, the Chancellor of the University, made the presentation.

Perhaps the most significant event of 1968 for us was the Parliamentary Farewell to Sir Alexander on February 28, at Gordon House, which we both attended. All the Members of the House of Representatives and the Senate were there when the resolution was moved to record the Parliament's appreciation of Sir Alexander Bustamante's twenty-three years of unbroken service. Glowing tributes were paid by Norman Manley, then Leader of the Opposition, Prime Minister Hugh Shearer, Florizel Glasspole, Edwin Allen, L.G. Newland, Robert Lightbourne and Edward Seaga. It was a very touching ceremony and the Chief's last visit to Parliament. Later that year, the Bustamante Foundation was launched simultaneously in four countries as a permanent and lasting memorial for his services to Jamaica. The headquarters of the Foundation are in London and our friend, Victor Page, has been Chairman since its inception. He and his wife Evelyn have been our good friends for many years and they come to Jamaica every February to celebrate the Chief's birthday on February 24 and to attend the annual Bustamante Lectures, including the Lady Bustamante Lecture, and then they stay on for my birthday.

When Bustamante was asked what particular area he would like to benefit from the Foundation, he unhesitatingly replied that his first choice would be to have students awarded scholarships, preferably in the field of medicine. He also made it quite clear that he did not wish to have any award named after him. The suggestion was taken up and

Dr Aubrey McFarlane began his most useful work as the first Chairman of the Scholarship Selection Committee along with Dr Ronald Irvine and Dr Jeffrey Wilson. So far, some sixty students have benefited from the Foundation. All have done exceedingly well in medicine, most of them gaining first-class honours.

Also in 1968, Sir Alexander and I attended the reopening of the old Olivier Bridge in St Thomas, linking Morant Bay with western St Thomas. Originally it had been named after Sir Sydney Olivier, once a Governor of Jamaica, but the imposing new bridge was named after Sir Alexander.

With 1969 came both sorrow and joy. Vividly I recall 2 September 1969. Soon after 1.00 p.m. when we had just finished lunch on the verandah, we received a telephone call to say that the Chief's cousin and life-long political associate and opponent, Norman Washington Manley, had just passed away. Sir Alexander was shocked and visibly moved. He said nothing for a while and then retired into his bedroom to lie down. Later in the afternoon, the television crew of JBC/TV and all the local media came up to Bellencita to interview him. Bustamante paid a moving tribute to this great statesman. The following day, we both visited Edna at Regardless and offered our profound condolences, together with a word of cheer. Sir Alex was not physically able to stand up to the rigours of the State Funeral, so I attended alone.

On September 15, the Gleaner's front page announced that both Sir Alexander Bustamante and Norman Washington Manley were to receive the nation's highest honour, that of National Hero, in recognition of the outstanding services they each had rendered to the nation. This was to take place on the first National Heroes Day, Monday, October 20, which was to be a Public Holiday.

The ceremony was held at Up-Park Camp. Prime Minister the Hon. Hugh Shearer received the General Salute on his arrival, and the Governor General, His Excellency, Sir Clifford Campbell, who was the Chancellor of the Order of National Heroes, drove majestically amid a cavalry escort onto the Parade Ground. The ceremony was ushered in by a military parade with all the traditional colour and glitter. The massed bands of the Jamaica Regiment, the Jamaica Defence Force and Constabulary, eight planes of the Jamaica Air Wing and the Air Squadron, joined in the parade and thrilled the thousands of spectators. The military display was accompanied by the conferring of the honour of National Hero on Sir Alexander and posthumously on Norman Manley. This honour entitles the recipient to be addressed as 'The Right Excellent'. With Sir Alexander and myself, were Mrs Edna Manley, widow of the late Hero, and her son Michael, the new Leader of the Opposition. The Military Ceremony concluded with a General Salute, a March Past, and three rousing cheers for the National Heroes of Jamaica. Sir Alexander is the only National Hero to have been so honoured during his lifetime.

Another high honour, and one which vividly brought memories back to me those turbulent years of the 1930s, was bestowed by Jamaica on Sir Alexander on the afternoon of Sunday, May 24, 1970. The occasion was the formal unveiling of the bronze statue of him, the work of Alvin Marriott, our famous Jamaican sculptor, which had been erected in the historic Victoria Park.

During the ceremony, Sir Alexander and I were seated in a special place of honour in front of the platform. As I glanced behind me, I could see the Leader of the Opposition, Michael Manley; his mother, Edna Manley; Vivian Durham; St William Grant (remarkable as usual in a military-type uniform); Lady Campbell; the Speaker of the House of Representatives, Eugene Parkinson; the General Secretary of the BITU, Edith Nelson; the Hon. Edward Seaga, one of the principal speakers at the ceremony; Prime Minister Hugh Shearer; and the Chairman of the National Trust Commission, Frank HIll. Thousands of persons attended, from leading national figures and diplomats to ordinary citizens, thronging the famous square and crowding the nearby railings of Victoria Park and the Kingston Parish Church. I can recall Eddie Seaga, under whose Ministry was the National Trust Commission, outlining in his address details of the plan to erect and unveil a similar statue of the Right Excellent Norman Washington Manley at the northern side of Victoria Park. The ceremony was to take place the following year on July 4, Mr Manley's birthday. I was very happy to attend that matching ceremony.

However, on the first occasion, I had the special pleasure and honour of unveiling the statue as the high point of the ceremony. When the moment came, I could hear the tremendous roar of applause and the sudden surge of excitement as I pulled away the Jamaican flag to reveal the life-size statue of Bustamante, standing on the pedestal where the statue of Queen Victoria had formerly been, captured by Marriott in the dramatic moment when the Chief emerged as the leader of the Jamaican workers in May 1938. His right hand is outstretched and the left is raised to his bare chest, recalling his famous words to the police, spoken at almost that very spot, "Shoot me, but leave my people alone!"

Although the Chief was living in retirement, he was far from being forgotten, as we were fully made to realise on Sunday, 19 October 1975, the day before National Heroes Day. Both Sir Alexander and I had been invited by the citizens of St Thomas, a parish with which we had close ties, to a reception at Blue Mahoe, Prospect. Coincidentally, this property adjoined our former home and property at Retreat. We set out from Bellencita for St Thomas in the Cadillac shortly after noon. Local residents had been made aware of our visit and, as the motorcade led by police outriders and followed by back-up police cars with flashing lights and sirens sounding, sped by, hundreds thronged the roadway just to have a glimpse of Bustamante, some waving, others clapping all together, giving a roar of acclamation as someone who had now apparently become a legend passed by. The women, in particular, looked especially happy as they shared the joy. This was the scene for almost the entire forty miles. It was absolutely incredible.

In Morant Bay, the motorcade stopped for a short while by the Court House as I stepped out of the car to lay a wreath from Sir Alexander at the foot of the statue of Paul Bogle, a mark of respect from one National Hero to another. The Hon. Isaac Matalon, Custos of St Thomas, extended the welcome. He jokingly recalled an incident many years before in which he had driven up in his vehicle to assist in pulling out Bustamante's car which had stuck while fording the Johnson River. Busta, with his usual fine humour, exclaimed in jest, "Stop, Moses, stop! If you come any nearer to me, I'll shoot you." The crowd roared with laughter. Other speakers included the Vice President of the BITU and former Prime Minister, Hugh Shearer. Opposition Leader Edward Seaga, in a moving address, reminded the audience of Sir Alex's impressive physical stature and distinguished looks, which made him stand out in any crowd. "When one becomes a National Hero," he said "we tend to lose sight of the other features which distinguish him from other men." The Party Leader continued, "Behind every great man there is a great woman. When we add up the stature of the man in charting the destiny of our country, a man who stands so high above his contemporaries, we must all the more give credit to his wife. Lady Bustamante stands out as a shining example of devotion to an individual and cause, the model of the dedicated Jamaican woman who by loyalty to her husband helped him to be great, and gave up the life that other woman would enjoy so as to make her husband great." And, referring to us both, he concluded, "May your names be long remembered by those born and those yet unborn."

On our return journey to Irish Town, Sir Alexander pulled up at spots along the road where a crowd had gathered, exchanging a quick word with the people who loved him so much. As we approached the Princess Margaret Hospital at Lyssons, a batch of nurses came out and flagged down the car determinedly, becoming something of a roadblock. As the car halted, they descended on Sir Aexander. He was absolutely delighted, as each one gave him a big hug and kiss and we drove on with lipstick heavily present on his collar and face. It was an outpouring of love and affection mixed with respect and admiration.

The following morning, National Heroes Day, Prime Minister Michael Manley with his wife Beverley paid us a visit at Bellencita, and appropriately so, to greet the National Hero. Michael repeated his earlier invitation to us to attend the 'Salute to the National Heroes' at the National Stadium later that same day. Sir Alex had not fully made up his mind to attend, possibly because of the late night he had in St Thomas. The Manleys, having completed their visit, left after spending an enjoyable time with us. Then, about an hour before the function was due to begin at the Stadium, the Chief suddenly decided that he wanted to go to the Salute. We hurriedly got ready and dressed and, without making it known that we were going to attend, headed in his custom-designed Cadillac for the National Stadium.

We entered the Stadium through the Marathon Tunnel of the Stadium. The moment Sir Alexander's presence was recognised and the TV and Radio crew announced that the new arrival appeared to be Sir Alexander in person, the roar of welcome that greeted his arrival shook the Stadium like an explosion. The tremendous crowd of some 35,000 was electrified. The people cheered loudly, stood in respect and excitedly stretched up on tip-toe to see the man whose name had been a force in Jamaica for over forty years. We pulled up and stopped in front of the Royal Box. For all those present and those who watched television at home, it was a historic occasion of national unity in which all Jamaica shared. The ceremony had just begun and all the dignitaries were seated. Governor General Sir Florizel Glasspole and his wife stepped down from the Royal Box and led the welcoming party to greet the National Hero in his car, with the rousing approbation of everyone present. They were immediately followed by Prime Minister and Sir Alexander's first cousin, Michael Manley, and Mayor of Kingston Ralph Brown and his wife. It was a stirring moment for me, filled with love, exemplified by warm embraces and kisses, and the cheers of the crowd. As usual, Sir Alexander did not overstay his welcome and left graciously, completing the circle of the Stadium so that everyone present could see him, retiring from the scene with the crowd echoing the sound of a Hero's welcome.

Another event that the Chief thoroughly enjoyed, although it was not such a grand occasion, was his ninety-second birthday party in 1976. It took place at the Denbigh Show Ground in Clarendon and was a very happy and popular celebration with crowds of well-wishers. It was there that we met Mike Henry for the first time, later to become a leading, dynamic member and deputy leader of the Party. Mr C.L.Stewart, an old friend now over ninety years old, was also present, along with Dr Abner Wright, late Custos of Clarendon.

When Sir Alexander retired to the St Andrew hills in 1967, he had already passed his eightieth birthday. Inevitably, the next ten years would bring signs of ageing and some ill-health but his mind remained alert and he followed public affairs with lively interest. The first Prime Minister to succeed him was Sir Donald Sangster, who had acted ably for Bustamante before his retirement. Unhappily, his term in office as Prime Minister lasted barely two months before he succumbed to an aneurysm in the brain. He always discussed important matters with Sir Alex before coming to a final decision and succeeding Ministers and Prime Ministers also came to Busta for counsel. I was regarded as the Chief Coordinator between my dear husband and his lieutenants. Since I am fortunate enough to have kept my good memory, I was able to help tremendously. He would turn to me in a discussion with a colleague and say, "Lady B., when did this happen and what were the circumstances?" and since I had also learnt from the Chief that brief and clear language was far more effective than a tedious and complicated reply, I could be of real assistance to him.

I always had good relationships with the other Prime Ministers from Bustamante's party, Hugh Shearer and Eddie Seaga. We had worked together on the same side of the political fence and our conversations could be lively, frank and constructive. Any ideas I had for improving social benefits for the poor always appeared to be welcome and they always seemed to be grateful to me for historical perspective which was one of the greatest gifts I inherited from Sir Alexander. And I have been fortunate that the Prime Ministers from the other party,

Michael Manley and P. J. Patterson, have always treated me with the utmost cordiality and trustworthiness, so my experience with them has been healthy, helpful and mutually beneficial.

Many visitors apart from politicians came to see Bustamante and, in spite of failing eyesight, he continued to enjoy the annual arrival of beauty queens coming to pay him their respects. Our friends such as Seragh and Effie Lakasingh and Ted and Monica Wells arranged lovely parties for our wedding anniversaries and birthdays which friends from abroad such as Dr Victor and Evelyn Page always managed to attend although they live in London. And there were quieter times when Sir Alex would sit for hours, listening while I played the piano or my Hammond organ. On other occasions, however, highly talented pianists and organists came and turned the living room of Bellencita into a concert hall. Among them I remember Eleanor Alberga-Bowes, Mike Thompson, Leslie Butler, Orrett Rhoden, Fay Lindo and the late Dorrit Baboolal.

Inevitably, the Chief's health fluctuated from time to time over the years, sometimes limiting his activities more than usual, but in 1977 some signs of deterioration began to appear. Following an attack of pneumonia at the close of 1976, complications had set in which warranted his hopitalisation in February of 1977 to ensure the best medical care together with professional nursing and proper equipment. After a few weeks in the Nuttall Hospital, where he was given the very best of care, he had recovered sufficiently to return home and I was indeed happy to have him back at Bellencita. His illness had been followed with great interest by thousands of persons at home and abroad and I was virtually beseiged by telegrams, letters and telephone calls from anxious enquirers. In spite of his frailty, Busta continued to take an interest in public affairs and he never lost the wit and humour that had always been among his great characteristics.

He received so much love, attention and care that it was incredible. During his last illness, Dr Karl Wilson-James, Dr Ronald Irvine and Dr Aubrey McFarlane were in attendance almost daily and they always made themselves available for consultation – something I always admired. Visiting at times were Dr McNaughton of Toronto General Hospital, Dr Joel McNair, formerly of Walter Reed Hospital, Drs John Sauer and Nancy Kester of New York and Dr Jerome Black, all showing the love and devotion they had for Sir Alexander. There were times, too, when Drs Lawson Douglas, Don Christian and Delevante were on hand to help.

There were frequent visits by the clergy of different denominations, one of them being the Reverend Cleve Grant. Several private masses were held at Bellencita by the then Roman Catholic Archbishop, Samuel Carter, and other priests such as Father Charles Judah and Father John Connolley, with many nuns attending.

My own spirits were bolstered by the presence of friends such as Evelyn Sangster who had worked with me in the BITU and Ena Mesquita, also a friend of the BITU, who would later become my secretary. And, of course, there were the Lakasinghs who have supported me in so many ways for so long, and Ivy Page-Brown, Joyce Robinson, Olga Beckford and Pearl Jordan McLean. Then there was Miss Vie. We have known each other since she was five years old and we grew up together in the countryside. She was my only woman friend to be at my wedding. Together they all made it possible for me to endure the stress and anxiety I suffered during my husband's illness. I owe so much to them and to my dedicated staff of Lena and Nellie, Edna and the late Cecil Barrett. They stood faithfully by me and so did my drivers, Sergeants Lawrence and Charles Purser, the late 'Timoshenko', and Sergeant Lewis and Officer McKitty.

On the anniversary morning of Jamaica's Independence, August 6, 1977, after the Chief had taken a light breakfast, Evelyn Sangster-Clarke and I helped him to his chair on our bedroom patio, facing the hills and valleys he loved so well. He kept gazing quietly into the distance as if in deepest contemplation. He began to snooze, and I took him to bed and made him comfortable. Shortly afterwards, he suddenly began to perspire profusely and turned pale. His pulse-beat became erratic, then with one great heave and a sigh, he laid down the burdens of ninety-three years, five months and two weeks, and passed peacefully away. I was paralysed with grief at his sudden passing, and as I recovered to face reality, I gave way to uncontrollable tears and a feeling of emptiness came over me. He, whom I had loved with all my heart, was gone, never to return.

After I had recovered from the first shock of the Chief's passing, with the help of the friends around me, I gradually became aware that all the radio stations had begun to play solemn music. The whole nation was grieving with me and the solemn music continued during the period of national mourning. Before long, Prime Minister Michael Manley with his mother, Edna, and his wife, Beverly, together with other members of their family had come to offer their condolences and from then on there was a steady stream of visitors wishing to express their sorrow and to console me. I knew that Bustamante's death was not alone my personal loss but one in which many thousands shared. He had led a good and noble life, full of devotion to his fellowmen and to his country. I will never forget the dignity and solemnity of Sir Alexander's State Funeral on Sunday, August 14, 1977, with which the nation paid him a farewell tribute, a sincere farewell to a true hero.

After the funeral, I was tempted to withdraw into a quiet, private life. But it was not to be. I could not leave my work with the BITU, The Union had been a great part of the Chief's life and it was my life too. The good friends who had supported me all through Busta's illness confirmed me in the idea that I still had a duty to him to carry on his work as far as I could. They also made me realise that I could make a contribution in my own right. But it was a call from outside Jamaica that made me fully aware that I had a part to play in public life. An invitation arrived for me to attend a Memorial Service for Sir Alexander at Westminster Abbey, to be held on Saturday, September 24. I could not refuse. I left Jamaica on September 21, travelling unaccompanied for the first time in my life. Once I reached London, I had the support of my friends there and I shall never forget the moving and beautiful service in the Abbey attended by so many Jamaicans from all walks of life. My friend Evelyn Page insisted that I should have a little holiday in Scotland before returning and on the way home I stopped in New York with relatives and friends.

As soon as I was home, I had to decide what I would do. Apart from my involvement with the Party, in an informal way, and the BITU, there were other areas where I had always been active, such as the Bustamante Hospital for Children and the Women's Club which offered a wide range of services. But now I began to be involved in the Bustamante Foundation and the Bustamante Institute of Public and International Affairs, the brainchild of Hector Wynter. Then there were various Service Clubs, Women Inc., the FISH Project, founded by the late Professor Louis Grant, and the Jaycee's 'Nuggets for the Needy' Charity, one which the Chief specially supported. There are constant calls on my time for fund-raising and good causes and I try to help wherever I can, but my diary is often full.

However, I try to find time for my home and garden, especially my orchids and anthuriums and the lychee trees. I have always grown vegetables and recently I have begun coffee cultivation. I still play the piano and the Hammond organ and, occasionally, my guitar or the accordion. Music is an integral part of my life. And I love to drive or, more often these days, be driven. The Chief taught me how to appreciate good cars, and since I did most of the driving in our early days, from end to end of Jamaica, it is a lesson that I have never forgotten.

One good personal development that grew out of the years after the Chief's death was the friendship that gradually developed between

Edna Manley and myself. Of course, we had known each other for years, but as the widows of two National Heroes, we were often together in the eye of the public. Naturally, we became closer and during the celebrations for 'Jamaica 21' in 1983 we kept in close touch as we attended many events to mark the historic occasion. After that, we saw each other frequently. Her death on 10 February 1986, was a severe blow for me and for our country which has lost a daughter who made a unique contribution to its history and culture.

Nineteen-eighty three was a particularly busy year. Not only did I attend many of the celebrations for 'Jamaica 21' but I also went to London to attend a service in Westminster Abbey to commemorate the twenty-first Anniversary of Jamaica's Independence and to mark the forty-first Anniversary of the release of Sir Alexander from Up-Park Camp. After the service, a reception was held in my honour at the Jamaican High Commission in London.

The following year, 1984, marked the Centenary of the birth of Sir Alexander. There was a year-long celebration by all Jamaica, and I attended most, if not all, of the events. How can I forget that crowd of several thousands who had gathered in the night on the actual date, February 24, at the Lucea Square in Hanover, following the ceremony at his birthplace at Blenheim. They had come to the town square to be entertained and to listen to the tributes paid to their founding father and fellow parishioner. On the same day, newspapers were filled with tributes from leaders and governments all over the world. The first of these came from the Prime Minister of India, Mrs Indira Ghandi herself, and it was delivered to me the night before at Bellencita by Mr Ram Lal, the Indian High Commissioner to Jamaica, in person, a gentleman for whom I have great respect.

Once again, I found myself at Westminster Abbey, this time for the Thanksgiving Service for Sir Alexander's Centenary. It was a very special occasion for me and Jamaicans in London, and elsewhere, turned out in full force. Outside the Abbey after the service there was a huge lingering crowd waiting to greet me, some requesting my signature on programmes and autograph books. Friends and associates were meeting and greeting with warm hugs and kisses.

Two years later, I was in London once more, but not at the Abbey. The Commonwealth Institute had invited me to be an official guest at their 'Caribbean Focus '86' celebration. This exposition was intended to make people more aware of the culture of the Caribbean and to broaden their outlook on the region, and cultural groups were invited to perform in Britain during the summer of 1986. I had the pleasure of being the special guest at the performance of our own Jamaica National Dance Theatre Company at the Institute on August 9. It was exciting to hear the tremendous reception the Company had from the audience and to read the appreciative reviews in the press. And it was exciting to see just how far the company started by Rex Nettleford and Eddy Thomas at Independence had gone. As always on these visits, my friends found out where I was staying and came to persuade me to leave the hotel and be their house guest. This was a lovely way to keep in touch with my friends abroad.

During the 1980s, something of a tradition had begun to grow up, having to do with my birthday. Every year when my birthday was approaching my close friends and members of the BITU, the JLP the Bustamante Foundation and the Bustamante Institute of Public and International Affairs would ask me what I would like to have done to mark the day. I would try to dissuade them from organising any big event, but I always failed miserably. If I took a firm stand, they would find a way of getting around me and, by planning behind my back, they would give me a surprise. In 1987, on a 'special' birthday, I was in for a grand surprise.

I was asked by Effie and Seragh Lakasingh to go down to their home in Cherry Gardens early in the afternoon to rest and then dress there in preparation for being taken out to dinner that night. I was looking forward to a quiet birthday dinner. When I was ready and stepped outside the house, I was greeted by a multitude of friends who sang *Happy Birthday* to a beautiful live organ accompaniment.

This was indeed a great surprise and a great party. Governor General Sir Florizel Glasspole, who also spoke, headed the list of guests. L.G.Newland was also there, celebrating his birthday on the same day as mine. Several touching tributes were paid to me. Mitsy Seaga, accompanied by her daughter Annabelle, spoke on behalf of her husband and herself. Michael Manley's message was read by his daughter Sarah. Joining me in the cutting of the cake were Michael's daughters, Sarah and Natasha. On conclusion of the toasts, with Eddie Shoucair as Chairman, I replied thanking Effie and Seragh for a wonderful evening and the guests for coming, mentioning the actress Madge Sinclair and my friends from Indiana, Winston and Joyce Chen-Sue.

What I do like about these birthday celebrations is that they afford all of us with the opportunity to catch up with good friends and long-time associates, from all levels. Unfortunately, we are unable to see or visit one another as often as we would like, but I find that occasions such as these help us all to keep in touch.

If 1987 had been a special and a happy year, 1988 was an entirely different experience. The events of that year are completely overshadowed by Hurricane Gilbert which swept through the island in the middle of September. No part of the island escaped completely but the hills were badly hit. Bellencita was not to be spared. The building suffered severe damage, in face, it was almost demolished. All the furnishings and fixtures were destroyed. Many of my treasured trees, including some of the lychees, were brought down and not one of them had a single leaf left on a branch after the storm passed, but I did not despair. I started rebuilding immediately, determined to have everything back as it had been originally and to return to live there as soon as was humanly possible. In the meantime, my good friends the Lakasinghs took me into their Cherry Gardens home as a house guest on an indefinite stay. But I wasted no time. I was on the Bellencita site daily from early morning to late afternoon, supervising the workmen myself to ensure that the structure would be stronger for the future and that the work was thoroughly done. By June of the following year, the rebuilding had reached the stage where I and my staff could live there once more. When the work was finally completed, Bellencita was just as it had been when the Chief and I had first moved in.

Looking back at the years between 1989 and now, I realise that I have begun to slow down somewhat. Although I still go down to the BITU almost every weekday, I am also reserving more time for myself, partly because the years are passing and partly as a result of an accident that happened a few years ago. For holidays I go on a cruise with friends, a very relaxing way of taking a break. And I think I enjoy them because they remind me of those sea voyages I made so often with the Chief to England or New York.

Then I look further back to August 1977, and realise that twenty years have passed since I lost my dear husband. In those years he has had ever-increasing recognition, In addition to the events I have mentioned there have been the dedication of the Bustamante Monument at the National Heroes Park on May 24, 1981, and the restoration of his birthplace at Blenheim as a National Shrine together with a museum, opened at the beginning of this year. I think of the awards which I have received: the Order of Jamaica, at a special ceremony at King's House on February 24, 1982; the Gleaner Company's Special Merit Award for Outstanding service to the Nation, on July 2, 1984; and Woman Inc.'s Celebration of Womanhood Award in 1988, 'In recognition of outstanding achievements which continue to inspire and encourage others to a Pursuit of Excellence', and many more. These awards make me feel that I have indeed, to some extent, kept my promise to continue his work as well as I could.

Whatever I have achieved, I could not have done without the support of my very good friends. Nor could I have succeeded without the staff at the Union office, and here I single out St Clair Shirley, one of the executives of the BITU over the years. He was responsible for the design and supervision of the Extension Wing of the present BITU Headquarters at Duke Street. He has always guided well in matters on which I sought his expertise. Indeed, his family can be regarded as an extension of our own family. My faithful secretaries over the years have helped to lessen my burdens and have made life easier for me as have my devoted staff.

I do not believe that God's gift to me could have been greater than that which made my life so full of concern for others, knowledge of how to improve their lives and energy with which to give them whatever help was possible. I strongly believe that it was God's decision that I should link my life with Sir Alexander Bustamante, for through him, I have been able to do everything possible to contribute in my simple way to creating a better life for the people of my country.

From time to time, I have been asked if I regret having had no children of my own. Both Sir Alexander and I had a deep love for children. I remember that he said, 'The youth of a nation are the trustees of posterity'. Although we had no children of our own, I must confess to mothering many. Even within the walls of Bellencita, even up to the present day, probably unknown to many, there have been protegés of mine. I have been godmother to more than fifty children and have raised some of them myself. Some are successful adults and some are nearby, even as I write. I rejoice that I have had the opportunity to help them individually while I tried to serve my country. I have had pleasure in seeing my 'children' flourish and make their own contribution to society. If growing up with me has been half the fun and satisfaction for them that it has been for me, I will go to my Maker with a clear conscience and the same happy disposition that has marked my days on earth